Steamer Crescent
.... July 8th..

Dear Brother
                    I wrote ... 29th
New York, of my hasty departure for
Tomorrow I expect to reach Chagres,
with no detention at Panama, shall re[ach]
by middle of August. This vessel saile[d]
alt[er] — & by hard work I got aboard a
before she left the dock — I was so mu[ch]
that I had no time for reflection, regr[et]
although I felt some when fairly emb[arked on]
my voyage — but now I have recove[red]
spirits, & feel more sanguine of succe[ss]
before I started, I have enjoyed excellen[t]
& we have had but one warm day s[ince I]
left New York, & that was soon afte[r]
the sun's line — now we are going [toward]
the sun & the weather will not gr[ow]
as you might supposed. I have a s[teerage]
passage on this vessel for which I p[aid]
& Steerage ticket on the Pacific side
I paid $150. — the expense of crossi[ng]

To Eleanor and Taylor Reese
with much love
August 25th
            Virginia Churchill McKenzie
                        Smith

Fortunes Are for the Few

LETTERS OF A FORTY-NINER

Nº 1.

Received   149.

Steamer Crescent City
Sunday 8th July 1849

Dear Brother

I wrote you on 29th June from
New York, of my hasty departure for California.
Tomorrow I expect to reach Chagres, & if I meet
with no detention at Panama, shall reach Cal—
by middle of August. This vessel sailed on 30th
ult— & by hard work I got aboard a few minutes
before she left the dock— I was so much hurried
that I had no time for reflection, regrets &c, &
although I felt some when fairly embarked on
my voyage— but now I have recovered my
spirits, & feel more sanguine of success than
before I started, I have enjoyed excellent health,
& we have had but one warm day since we
left New York, & that was soon after we crossed
the sun's line— now we are going south from
the sun & the weather will not grow warmer
as you might suppose. I have a steerage
passage on this vessel for which I paid $80.—
& steerage ticket on the Pacific side for which
I paid $150.— the expense of crossing the
Isthmus is not included in either of the above

Letter of Charles William Churchill to Mendal Churchill,
July 1849, written aboard the steamer Crescent City.

Fortunes Are for the Few

LETTERS OF A FORTY-NINER

By

Charles William Churchill

EDITED BY

DUANE A. SMITH & DAVID J. WEBER

San Diego Historical Society
1977

*Library of Congress Catalog Card Numbers 77-76134
ISBN: 0-918740-00-2*

*Designed and printed by Grant Dahlstrom at The Castle Press,
Pasadena, California*

Table of Contents

List of Illustrations

Introduction

Twenty-six-year-old Charles William Churchill of Lawrence County, Ohio, whose letters comprise this book, was among the thousands of Anglo-Americans who sought their fortunes in the newly discovered gold fields of California in 1849. Perhaps as many as three-fourths of the forty-niners journeyed to California by land, but Charles Churchill joined the minority who took the more rapid, secure, and expensive sea route to the Pacific Coast, going by way of Panama. Like most forty-niners, Churchill left home with high expectations which were never realized in California. His ambition led him to join an unusual expedition to prospect in northwestern Mexico in 1851, but he returned poorer than when he left. Settling in California near Mariposa, Churchill abandoned mining, took up storekeeping, and thought of returning to Ohio. Apparently he also took to heavy drinking as his prospects grew bleaker. He died in 1855 in California, far from family and friends.

Charles Churchill described his hopes and his frustrations in the letters he wrote from California to his family in the East. The letters were written without any thought of publication. Indeed, they would have been lost entirely had they not been carefully preserved by his younger brother Mendal, to whom most of them were addressed.

Like Charles, Mendal Churchill considered going to California. Instead, he did not go far from home to seek and make his fortune. In 1850, at the age of twenty-one, he moved from Lawrence County, in southeastern Ohio, where he was born, to Keystone Furnace in nearby Jackson County. There, during the years that his brother's prospects diminished in California, Mendal prospered. He worked his way up from storekeeper to bookkeeper, and finally, in 1854, became manager of an iron smelter, or "furnace." With the outbreak of the Civil War, Mendal Churchill enlisted in the army as a private and rose quickly through the ranks. At the end of the War he was brevetted Brigadier General of the U. S. Volunteers for meritorious service, especially in the Battle of Atlanta in which he sustained a minor wound. Returning to Ohio after the war, he settled at Zanesville, some sixty miles east of Columbus, where he became president of the Ohio Iron Company in 1866, a position he held until 1891, along with numerous civic and business-related positions.[1]

When he retired in 1891, General Churchill set out on a world tour which eventually brought him to the Pacific Coast. Impressed with San Diego, he bought property in Coronado, where he built a splendid home at 1308 Orange Avenue on the corner of Churchill Place, which still bears his name. He moved into his new home in 1895, and apparently brought with him from Ohio a packet of Charles' letters marked "Letters from my brother who died in Merced County, California in 1855." General Churchill was a meticulous record keeper, and it was an awareness of history as well as affection for his brother that prompted him to have a typescript made of much of the letter in which Charles described his mining ventures in northern Mexico.

When General Churchill died in San Diego in 1902, his brother's letters were stored in a trunk with papers from the

Civil War, destined to be forgotten for seventy years. Along with most of his possessions, the trunk of papers passed on to a niece, Mary Churchill Pratt, whom Mendal Churchill and his wife had adopted.[2] Miss Pratt later married Bernard Wright McKenzie, and when she died in 1912, the trunk became the property of their daughter, Virginia McKenzie Smith. In 1972 when Mrs. Smith was preparing to move from her home in San Diego she began to sort through the contents of General Churchill's letters. She recognized their importance and presented them to the San Diego Historical Society where they form part of the Churchill Collection.

A large number of people helped in the production of this book: Sandra Gustafson, Gregg Hennessey and Rosemarie McLain of San Diego; Cynthia Radding de Murrieta of the Centro Regional del Noroeste in Hermosillo, Sonora, Mexico; Joe Park of the University of Arizona, Tucson; Bertha Schroeder of Mariposa, California; and Barbara Lujan of Durango, Colorado.

In editing Charles Churchill's California letters, we have added or changed punctuation occasionally to make sentences more intelligible. We did not, however, want to destroy the flavor of the original letters so we left eccentric spellings of words such as *probaly*, *untill*, and *their*, when Churchill meant to write *there*. Churchill's spelling was reasonably accurate, although he consistently misspelled Mendal's name as Mendall. To facilitate the reading of these letters, we have prepared brief descriptions of members of the Churchill family, which appear in the appendix.

DUANE A. SMITH
Fort Lewis College, Durango, Colorado

DAVID J. WEBER
Southern Methodist University, Dallas, Texas

1. This biographical information has been drawn from vol. VI of *The Historical and Biographical Cyclopaedia of the State of Ohio* (Cincinnati: Western Biographical Publishing Co., 1849), and the Military Order of the Loyal Legion of the United States, Commandery of the State of Ohio, Circular no. 33, Series of 1902, *In Memoriam: Companion Mendal Churchill.* A typescript of the former and a facsimile of the latter are in the Churchill Collection at the San Diego Historical Society. We have also relied upon interviews with Virginia Churchill McKenzie Smith.

2. Mary Churchill Pratt's mother, Elizabeth Loughry, was the sister of General Churchill's wife, Mary Loughry (1836-1886). General and Mrs. Churchill had no children of their own.

I

CHARLES CHURCHILL

1822-1849

"I am willing to go any place that money can be made"

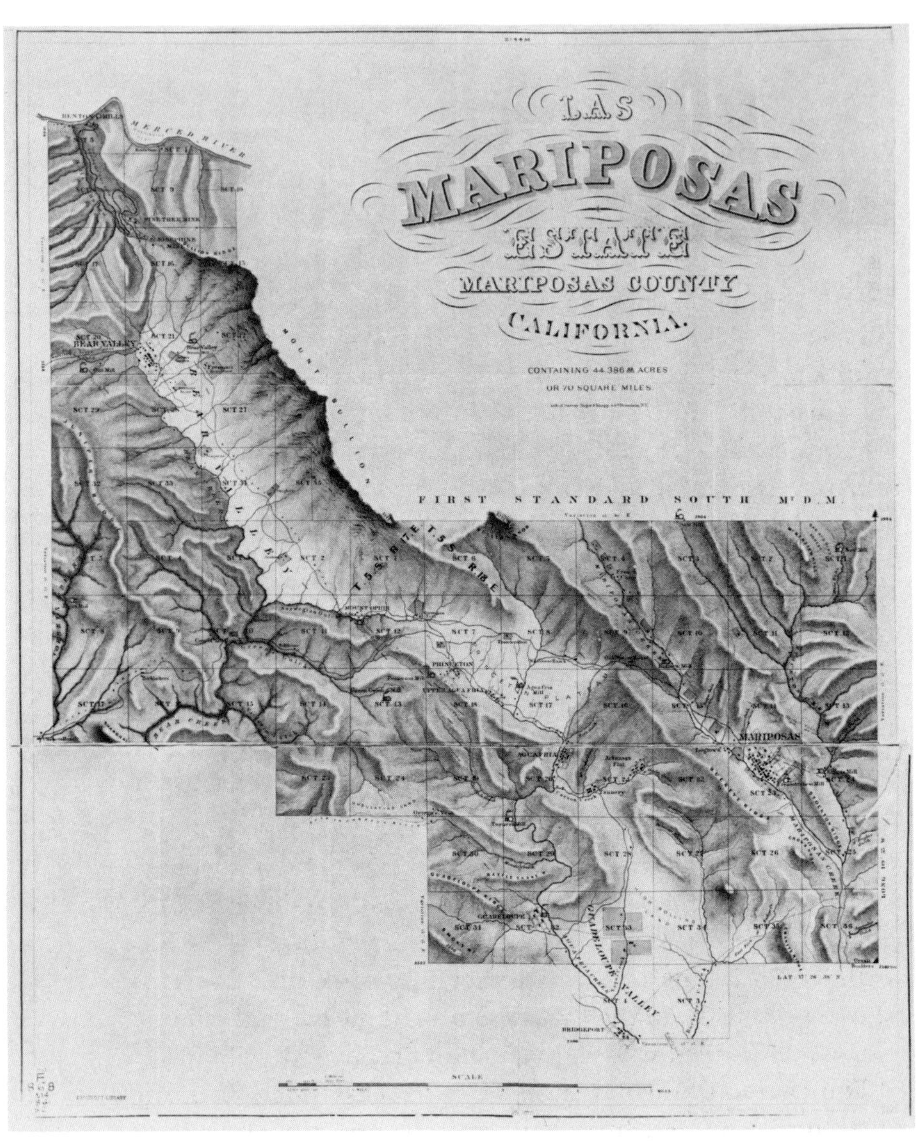

"Las Mariposas Estate, 1861." Reproduced through the courtesy of the Bancroft Library.

THE FORTY-NINER MINER has emerged as part of western folklore and legend — indomitable in spirit, restless in temperament, and prodigal in life. He followed the golden star that lured the multitudes to California and the West in the generation after 1849. Outstanding success did not characterize his career, although a few fortunate ones found their personal "El Dorado." But whether they succeeded or failed, these legendary forty-niner prospector-miners opened and developed much of the mining West. Marking their paths today are abandoned mines, forgotten mining districts, and shells of the camps where they once worked and played.

No one knew what the future held, only that it was golden, in that winter of wonders, 1848-49, when news of the California gold discoveries reached all sections of the United States and spread throughout the world. It was then that the decision had to be made — to go or to stay. Did one choose to remain at home, where the future could be more easily charted, or did one cast his fortune on the unknown California with its far more attractive opportunities? Perhaps 80,000 persons from the United States alone chose the latter course and headed westward by land and by sea.

The choice could not have been an easy one; it meant breaking home ties, uprooting oneself, and traveling long distances to the gold fields. An unknown destiny awaited. The young, single American male could migrate most easily and thus comprised a large segment of the forty-niners. Most forty-niners knew little or nothing about actual mining methods, but possessed supreme confidence that they could master the necessary skills. The motley procession included doctors, farmers, lawyers, blacksmiths, clerks, teachers, the skilled and the unskilled from all walks of life.

In that great throng trying to reach California was a twenty-six-year-old Ohio native, Charles William Churchill. He was one of the fortunate ones who neither turned back nor "put down roots" in a grave along the way. But he was convinced, as were the others, that California would provide the wealth he had been seeking, after which he could return home, settle down to a respectable life, and turn to other pursuits.

Churchill's career prior to 1849 was not unusual for a young man of his time. His father had migrated to Ohio from Massachusetts and his mother from New York. They had been married in 1818 when Ohio still contained vestiges of a frontier land; Indian raids and the War of 1812 remained fresh in their memories. Charles was the second child and eldest son of this union, which produced six children, all born in Lawrence County in the southeastern corner of the state along the Ohio River.

Charles Churchill grew up on a farm and attended the nearby country school. The education he received was average for the day, his spelling, punctuation, and grammar displaying the common weaknesses of his background. His father died in March, 1835, leaving his mother to raise the rest of the family, only two of whom were over ten at the time. As early as 1839 or 1840, Churchill apparently went to work as a store clerk, an occupation in which he is found when his letters commence.

Solomon Churchill, born in Plymouth, Massachusetts, 1788; died in Lawrence County, Ohio, 1835. Father of Charles William Churchill and Mendal Churchill. Photograph courtesy of Mrs. W. Murray Smith.

Little of his early life can be reconstructed beyond these few skimpy facts. Not until 1842 were his letters saved by his brother Mendal. At that time Charles was on his way from New York (where he apparently had some connection with his uncle, William Churchill) to Augusta, Georgia, where he was going to be employed. Almost all the letters included herein were sent to Mendal; the brothers seemed to be very close. Mendal had been born in 1827, the second son, and Charles must have felt an obligation to be a substitute father to his brother. By 1842 Mendal had attended the local country school and either had spent, or would soon spend, two terms at an academy at Burlington. To raise money for the family he was employed at a local country store, undoubtedly following in Charles' footsteps.

The first letter in the Churchill Collection is dated February 27, 1842, and was sent from Augusta to "Mr. E. B. Greene, Greene's Store, Lawrence Co. Ohio." Elisha Greene had married Charles' older sister, Elizabeth, in 1838. On his first long trip from Ohio, Charles tells his brother-in-law what he saw and much about himself. The letter is quoted in its entirety not only because of its position, but also because, as someone proudly noted above the main text, "This is a pretty fair descriptive letter for a 19 year old."

Augusta Feb 27th 1842

Dear Brother

You will be supprised to receive a letter from me, dated at this place, as I have not in my letters to you mentioned anything about my intention to leave New York for a short time. Mr. [William] Churchill obtained a situation for me in this place for the winter in a crockery store. I left New York on the 27th last month in company with Mr. Churchill & family, who came on to Washington City, the capitol U.S. We left New York in the morning and arrived at Philadelphia about 3 o'clock. It was very windy and I lost my cap while passing from one car to the other, but succeeded in borrowing an old hat untill I arrived at Philadelphia, and bought me a cap and returned my borrowed hat by the railroad. We stoped all night in Philadelphia, and started the next morning at 8 o'clock for Baltimore in the cars, and arrived at 3 o'clock, took dinner, and left for Washington at which place we arrived a little after dark, and engaged lodging at a private boarding house. In the morning before breakfast William and I took a walk to the capitol, which is situated on a hill above most of the town. That is to say, the town is built on two plains, and I may almost say all of the town is on the lower one and when you are standing at the capitol you have a very good view of the town. It is quite a large building and surrounded by an iron railing perhaps a mile around and the ground enclosed is laid out in walks, with trees, shrubbery, etc. and has a pretty appearance in the spring. In the center of the building under the cupola is a large circular room (The Rotunda), and large paintings hanging against the wall: The Battle of Saratoga, Yorktown, Declaration of Independence, Annapolis, a full length portrait of H. Clay and a splendid painting representing the Baptism of Pocahontas.[1] We also saw Greenough's statue of Washington. It is raised to the height of twenty feet (perhaps more and perhaps less I will not be certain about the height), on a square colum or pillar, made of square blocks of granite. The statue is twelve feet high from the stone on which the feet rest and is in a sitting posture.[2] We also went to the Senate Chamber and House of Representatives, both of these are in the form of a half circle, the Senate of course being much smaller than the House. At twelve Mr & Mrs C William and self went to the House with the expectation of hearing Mr Adams from Mass, but were disappointed. A Mr Sprigg[3] from Kentucky was speaking upon the Treasury Note Bill as I found out after listening for some time. He made a three hour speech full of oaths that would of done credit to the most profane swearer, and although his subject was the "TNB" he did not confine his remarks to that particular subject, but to everything and nothing in particular. I think it is a disgrace to the country that such a man is allowed to take his Seat in our Halls of Legislation. The next day being the Sabbath, I went to hear Mr Moffit, the Chaplain of the House, and in the afternoon walked to the President's House, which is about 1½ miles from the Capitol. Pennsylvania Avenue, the principal street, runs from the capitol to the P. House. It is a good size building (very definite description) painted white, and on the back part, or that which faces the Capitol is laid out in walks etc. On Monday went with Mr C & William to see the Patent Office, Post Office and President, but that not being his day for receiving company, did not see him. On Tuesday morning before daylight I left Washington for Fredericksburg, Va. At twelve left the latter place in the cars for Richmond, the capitol of Virginia, and arrived at about 4 o'clock. What I saw of that place did not give me a very favourable opinion of it. The streets were very muddy, and no sign of a pavement, or anything like business. I was informed though by a resident, the part I saw was the worst part of the town, and that there was a considerable business done there etc. I left that afternoon for Petersburgh in the cars distant 22 miles, and from the latter place to Weldon in N. Carolina, and arrived at 2 o'clock in the morning. The cars were waiting for us, and we left immediately for Wilmington N.C. and arrived about 3 o'clock on Wednesday, having travelled from Fredricksburgh Va to Wilmington N. Carolina by Railroad. At Wilmington took a steam boat for Charleston S.C. and arrived at 9 o'clock on Thursday morning. There is a railroad from Charleston to Augusta Geo which leaves at 7 in the morning, and of course I was obliged to remain untill Friday morning. I arrived at Augusta on the same afternoon distant from Charleston 136 miles. I am in John G Dunlap's Store and boarding in his family. I expect to remain about 4 months. I receive at the rate of $700 a year and pay my expenses to and from this place. I am obliged to close my letter for the want of room. Please show this letter to Mother. Give my love to Betsey and kiss your son for me. And tell Melissa, Mendal, Julia and Solomon, and above all Mother I did not forget them. I am very anxious to hear from you and hope you will loose no time, and write to me immediately. Direct to the care J G Dunlap Augusta Geo

Your Most Aff Brother
C. W. CHURCHILL

9

DURING the next 26 months Charles sent his brother Mendal at least seven letters from Augusta. His strong concern for his mother, brothers, and sisters continued, Churchill always trying to send them money or apologizing for not being able to do so. He then went to Buffalo, New York, but returned to Augusta by June, 1845. Only two letters remain from this second sojourn. In fact, from September, 1845, to February, 1848, no letters are known to exist, leaving a tantalizing gap. When the letters resume, Charles reemerges in Buffalo.

Considering his fairly lengthy residence in Augusta, his comments on the South and his impressions of slavery are few. On July 6, 1842, he wrote Mendal, "I went last Friday July 1st to see a negro man hung for murder & it was truly a warning to all such as feel tempted to commit that dreadful crime." The slave had been converted to Catholicism shortly before his execution, and Charles added, with a touch of humor, "Whether the man to whom the negro belonged will pay to have masses said to keep the poor fellow out of purgotory is more than I can say but it is a debatable question in my mind he being a staunch Presbyterian." This was his only comment on the South's peculiar institution; perhaps this Buckeye from the border region was not shocked by what he saw.

He was impressed by the Southerners, who "kept up the Fourth of July in a manner suitable to the occasion. Not by getting drunk." Unfortunately, his first business failed to prosper and it was closed by auction. Writing his brother after this event, Churchill expressed the philosophy which motivated him throughout his life: "I have no idea where I will go to, but I am willing to go anyplace that money can be made." Typical American that he was, he was forever looking for a position that paid more and offered more chance for advancement. Soon after his first arrival in Buffalo, he confessed that he was seeking a job in Cincinnati to be nearer home, "not with much prospect of success." He clerked at a Buffalo store, as he did when he returned to the South. In Augusta he apparently held a managerial position or was an owner, because he hired a clerk to assist him.

On June 23, 1845, after complaining of business being slow, Charles found time to answer Mendal's inquiry as to when he planned to "leave this world of single blessedness and get married." In his reply Churchill showed much of his personal feelings toward life.

> "I would say most emphatically, that I do, but at some future time, certainly not within a few years for several very good and sufficient reasons. In the first place my affairs at present are not in a condition to allow of my indulging in the expence necessary to a right enjoyment of the marital state. Secondly I wish to see a little more of the world before I settle for life. Or in other words I wish to travel a little, at all events over the U.S., if not other countries. Thirdly I have serious doubts whether I would be contented, but this last objection I most certainly should consider void as soon as I got in love."

He ended by assuming the role of surrogate father: "But [I] sincerely hope you have no idea of getting married yourself, if so I shall most positively object to anything of the kind. Twenty one is as early as any man ought to be married."

Mendal heeded his brother's advice, for he did not get married until November 28, 1861, long after the end of this story and three months after he had joined the 27th Ohio Volunteer Infantry during the Civil War.

Before he returned to Buffalo to clerk in a store in February, 1848, Churchill tried to find employment in New York but failed. He still hoped for a position in Cincinnati but seemed unwilling to gamble on going there without a job. Buffalo, on the other hand, apparently held out great opportunity. He wrote Mendal on February 16, "Buffalo is a pleasant place to reside in. . . . It will eventually be a great business place, its increase in population is unparalleled even in this great country of ours, where cities spring up in a day." Charles forecast Buffalo's future correctly; it would be for years one of the major cities on the Great Lakes.

Churchill continued to worry about his family, inquiring about his mother's activities, Solomon's education, and Mendal's future plans.

> "Have you thought anything about choosing a profession whereby to gain a living? . . . It is bad business working merely for your living. I speak from experience, having tried it for several years. I shall be able to save $250 a year from my salary & can loan you a small amount (say $50 or $75) if you can speculate to advantage with it. I am not *very rich, just at the present time*, for when I came here I only had money enough to defray my expenses, but I have saved some little since I have been here. . . . It is getting rich rather slowly, but at present I must be content with it."

Business reverses dogged Charles' career. The crockery and glassware firm for which he contracted to work a year failed in August, 1848, but the determined Churchill turned it to an advantage when he and a partner purchased the store and reopened August 12 as "Mulligan & Churchill." He even predicted that he had located permanently. Unfortunately, as he confessed to Mendal, neither partner had any capital and at present "the firm is not considered a very 'stiff one'." As the months passed, they kept it afloat. "With regard to my prospects, I can hardly hazard an opinion," he wrote in October; "[the firm] is doing as well as could be expected under the existing circumstances."

As the year ended, Charles Churchill's last in the East, rumors and actual evidence of the California gold discovery reached Buffalo. It is not known when he first heard of it, or even what happened to the firm of "Mulligan & Churchill," except that it closed. By May, 1849, Charles was in New York and made no mention of his Buffalo business.

His letters show him to have been a young man of ambition, who left home to seek his fortune but who also retained strong family ties. He was optimistic and determined, as shown by his Augusta and Buffalo experiences. His luck or skill, one cannot say which, had not been too great up to then, and he had suffered several reversals in his drive for financial independence. He admitted as much in his advice to Mendal back in February, 1848, so he was not unwilling to face the reality of his situation.

Charles Churchill continued to search for the quick road to fortune; he probably speculated on the side, as he offered to do with Mendal. He moved around a great deal, whether because of his own restless nature or his searching. This trait characterized him throughout life. His cousin, William Churchill, Jr., writing Mendal on November 22, 1851, had this to say, "I enclose a letter just received from Charles. He appears to have acted with little judgment in moving about so much. Two or three times he has been $400 ahead & spent the amount in making a new move."

Of his personal nature Churchill indicates little, except in his early letters. He seldom courted young ladies, it seems, nor did he drink much, if his comment on the July Fourth festivities indicates his true feelings. Without question he felt responsibilities toward his family, although he refused to take the risk of going to Cincinnati to look for work, which would have put him closer to home. Nor did he seem to be able to visit them, although they invited him on several occasions.

As the gold rush of 1849 unfolded, Charles William Churchill was in New York, not much farther advanced materially than seven years earlier, when he had left the same city for Augusta. But experience had been gained, maturity acquired. In the end it would be his choice whether to heed the alluring call of California. At first he hesitated, unsure as to what to do. Even as late as May 5, 1849, he told Mendal, "I have not yet decided what course I shall persue, perhaps that I may go to California, altho I do not think it very probable." Finally he decided to go, and we follow him now as he placed his tomorrows on the turn of the golden wheel of fortune, known as the California mother lode country.

NOTES

1. Some of these paintings still hang in the Capitol's rotunda. John Trumbull painted three of them: "Surrender of Lord Cornwallis at Yorktown," "Surrender of General Burgoyne at Saratoga," and "Declaration of Independence." John Chapman painted "Baptism of Pocahontas at Jamestown, Virginia."

2. Horatio Greenough (1805-52) has been described as the ablest American sculptor of his time. He carved from Italian marble a twenty-ton heroic statue of Washington scantily clad and seated on a throne. The sculpture created much controversy and was eventually moved to the Smithsonian Institution.

3. Representative James C. Sprigg served in the 27th Congress, 1841-43, from Kentucky. The Mr. Adams to whom Churchill referred was John Quincy Adams, sixth president, and since 1831 serving a distinguished career in the House.

II

TO CALIFORNIA VIA PANAMA

1849

"It is time I was accumulating something"

> I jumped aboard the 'Liza ship
> And traveled on the sea,
> And everytime I thought of home
> I wished it wasn't me!
>
> —"Oh, California," *Out West*

You are driven round the steerage like a drove of hungry swine,
And kicked ashore at Panama by the Independent Line;
Your baggage is thrown overboard, the like you never saw,
A trip or two will sicken you of going to Panama.

> —"Humbug Steamship Companies,"
> *Original California Songster*

Early view of San Diego.

J UNE OF 1849 found Charles Churchill in New York City, concerned about the two great contagions of his time and place: gold fever and cholera. Cholera had first swept across the United States in 1832-1834, then reentered the country from Europe in the winter of 1848-1849. By mid-May of 1849 cholera had taken the lives of some 5,000 New York- ers. Death came swiftly and terribly within a day or even a few hours after the first symptoms—diarrhea, vomiting, and cramps. The dreaded cholera edged westward from New York toward Churchill's family in Ohio in the spring of 1849, and Churchill was alarmed. Carried by his fellow forty-niners, cholera would follow Churchill to California.[1]

Churchill never contracted cholera, but gold fever hit him hard. By June 1849 he had succumbed completely to the lure of California's promised wealth. By that June, as one contemporary described it,

"About eight months had elapsed since the tidings of an Eldorado in the West reached the Atlantic shore. The first eager rush of adventurers was over, yet there was no cessation to the marvelous reports, and thousands were only waiting a few further repetitions to join the hordes of emigration."[2]

For those who could afford it, the sea routes offered the

surest way to get from the East Coast to the gold fields. Churchill hoped at first to book passage on a ship that would take him to California via Cape Horn at the tip of South America, a 13,000-mile voyage that took an average of six months. Demand for tickets on vessels headed 'round the Horn ran high, though, and as June slipped by Churchill could not readily obtain passage. At the end of the month, however, he had the good fortune to get tickets for the steamers which connected New York and San Francisco via Panama—the fastest route to California.

Steamer service connecting New York to the West Coast had begun late in 1848, spurred on by government subsidies to two private companies to carry the mail. In the Atlantic, steamships sailing for the United States Mail Steamship Company made their way from New York to the Chagres River in Panama in nine to eleven days. At the small and notoriously unhealthy village of Chagres, passengers were left on their own to hire a dugout canoe and boatmen to pole them nearly forty miles up the Chagres to Gorgona, a journey of three days. From Gorgona, travelers usually hired a horse or mule to make the twenty-mile journey to Panama City on the Pacific Coast. In the rainy season, when the trail was muddy, this one-day trip might take much longer, as Churchill discovered. At Panama City, travelers sought connections with a steamer from the Pacific Mail Steamship Company. Those steamers pushed northward to San Francisco in eighteen to twenty-one days, so the entire journey from New York via Panama might take a total of thirty-three to thirty-five days, with favorable conditions and good connections.[3]

Conditions were not always favorable, however, and

good connections could not be depended upon in 1849. The steamer service, still in its infancy, was not set up for large scale passenger service. No one could have anticipated the demands that the discovery of California gold would suddenly thrust upon the mail companies. As Americans frantically sought ways to get to California in the winter and spring of 1849, numerous other vessels not related to the mail service began to carry passengers from East Coast cities to Chagres. Churchill booked passage on one of these, the steamer *Crescent City*.

Such Argonauts as Charles Churchill, then, began to descend on Panama in large numbers in 1849, overtaxing limited facilities, especially in Panama City. Although numerous vessels were available to meet the demand for transportation from the Atlantic coast to Chagres, too few vessels plied Pacific waters to accommodate would-be miners headed for San Francisco. Many gold seekers then found themselves stranded in Panama City for weeks. When the Pacific mail steamer *Oregon* reached Panama City in February 1849, for example, some 1,200 people sought passage on that ship, although its capacity was about 250.[4] Churchill was fortunate to obtain a ticket on the Pacific mail steamer *Panama*, before leaving New York City. He waited in Panama City for only two weeks before shipping out. Without prior arrangements, he might have had to settle for passage on a sailing vessel out of Panama City. Beating north against prevailing winds and currents, those vessels were notoriously slow and forty-niners avoided them if possible. The Panama route, then, was potentially the quickest way to California, but in 1849 it was also fraught with uncertainty, delay, and danger on the unhealthy Isthmian crossing.

Churchill describes his journey from New York to San Francisco in the letters which follow. He provides fascinating details about many aspects of the journey, but neglects some matters which other travelers found memorable. Churchill did not get seasick, for example, but he must have seen miserable traveling companions such as A. G. Henderson, who recalled "the plunging steamer tossed about at the sport of waves, dozens of poor fellows hanging like myself to the iron posts, . . . and I could see first one, then another commence paying tribute to Neptune."[5]

New York 5th June 1849

My Dear Brother

Yours of 16th of May was received on 22nd inst. I should have written you before but I have not yet decided with regard to California matters.

I feel somewhat alarmed that the cholera should be so near you, but trust that it will not reach Burlington.

I have heard of a very simple remedy which has been tried in Chicago in a number of cases with eminent success.

It consists of 4 parts of sulphur and 1 part of charcoal made into pills about the size of a pea. The cholera is usually preceded by the diarreah, and on the first appearance of the diarreah take one of the above pills and so on for every two hours untill the diarreah is checked. When that is effectually done stop taking the pills. I have it from the best authority that this simple remedy has been fully tested in Chicago and has not failed in one case if taken when the disease first made its appearance in the form of diarreah and that it has cured cases far advanced, which would not yield to other remedies.[6]

You must be very careful of yourself—regular in your diet etc., and if you should have the diarreah, have it checked at once, for at present it is a premonitory symptom of the cholera. I recommend you to try the prescription of charcoal and sulphur—39 cases and 11 deaths reported here today of cholera. With regard to California, I am making preperations to leave about the 20th of this month, but will not probably get off that soon. I am going round the Cape. I do not expect to go digging gold immediately on my arrival, but I have every reason to think that I can obtain profitable employment immediately upon my arrival. I may perhaps join a company if I find one to suit me. I have not yet engaged my passage altho I have several vessels in view. I am waiting with the hope that something favorable will turn up.

You may think it strange perhaps that I have not yet made out Mother's account, but such is the case. Uncle's affairs are in such a situation that I fear that it will be almost impossible and then he has such an aversion to going into any kind of business. However I hope to be able to accompolish something relative to it. I regret to hear of Geiger and Nichols loss. What has Franklin done with his place? Hired it out to someone else[?] That black fellow appeared to be an honest hard working man. Sorry he died.

Barton I presume has not yet removed his family to the furnace? I shall write to him before I start for California. Does Mother enjoy good health? and where is she staying? I trust Betsey and Melissa are well. Julia I suppose is still at Proctorsville.[7] Has Uncle William Fritchard got home? If so did he get his money? I shall write you again in about 2 weeks, and in the mean time you must write to me very frequently, for I am somewhat alarmed at the cholera being in your neighbourhood.

I trust Mrs. Greene[8] has entirely recovered her health. Remember me to all. Tell Eddy to be a good boy or I will be "down on him" the first time I see him.[9] Hoping to soon hear from you.

Truly yours etc.
C. W. Churchill

P. S. I have not been able to find Bartons Note. I have no doubt however but it is somewhere in Uncles papers. There is no danger of its being in the hands of third parties.

Truly, etc.
C. W. Churchill

Mr. Mendal Churchill
Burlington
Lawrence County
Ohio

New York 29th June 1849

My Dear Brother

I was shocked at receiving a letter from you on 26th inst. written on 16th inst., conveying the melancholy intelligence of the death of James Wheeler.[10] So long a time had elapsed between your two letters that I felt quite confident that James was recovering and the intelligence was doubly melancholy.

I was also deeply greived to hear of Melissa's sickness but trust from the tone of your letter that it was not very serious.

I wrote Julia on 24th inst which I presume was duly received. I shall start for California tomorrow in the Crescent City.[11] I have a ticket for the other side and can hope, allowing for a reasonable delay, to reach California about middle of August or first of Sept. It was only at 4 o'clock this after-

Crescent City. In June 1849 Churchill booked passage from New York to Chagres on the Crescent City, a new wooden side-wheel steamer. Reproduced by permission of The Mariners' Museum, Newport News, Virginia.

noon that I learned that a ticket could be procured for the Pacific Steamer for July. Of course I availed myself of the opportunity at once. The tickets are in great demand, and it was purely accidental that I was able to obtain one. Thiere [there] is no difficulty in obtaining a passage on this side to Chagres. The great difficulty is on the other side.

I feel quite melancholy at the idea of going now the time is so short, but it cannot be prevented. I think it is my interest to go. I could obtain a situation here that would enable me to live, but that would not answer my purpose. At my time of life, it is time I was accumulating something and then the situation of Mother's affairs render it necessary that I should be in a situation to contribute something to the support of the family. I have not the time to write at length, so you must excuse this short letter. I can only bid you all a melancholy farewell, for I do feel quite bad at the idea of going so far from home, but it can't be helped. I shall write you either from Chagres or Panama, and of course when I arrive at Cal. I shall also write Barton by mail. Good-bye. God bless you all.

Truly yours,
C. W. Churchill

[P.S.]

You must pre-pay your letters to me else they will not reach me. Write me at San Francisco, Cal., about 18th July and it will probably reach me in about 2 months. Wm. [William Churchill, Jr.] says he would be very h[appy] to hear from you. You will see by my [letter to] Julia what course I decided to pursue [words missing] to mother etc. with Uncle.

Yours
C. W. Churchill

No. 1
Received   /49
[Apparently noted by Mendal Churchill]

Steamer Crescent City
Sunday 8th July 1849

DEAR BROTHER

I wrote you on 29th June from New York, of my hasty departure for California. Tomorrow I expect to reach Chagres, and if I meet with no detention at Panama, shall reach California by middle of August. This vessel sailed on 30th ult., and by hard work I got aboard a few minutes before she left the dock. I was so much hurried that I had no time for reflection, regrets, etc., although I felt some when fairly embarked on my voyage, but now I have recovered my spirits, and feel more sanguine of success than before I started. I have enjoyed excellent health, and we have had but one warm day since we left New York, and that was soon after we crossed the sun's line. Now we are going south from the sun and the weather will not grow warmer as you might supposed. I have a Steerage passage on this vessel for which I paid $80 and Steerage ticket on the Pacific side for which I paid $150.[12] The expense of crossing the Isthmus is not included in either of the above amounts. It will probably be about $30, provided I walk the greater part of the way. I left N. Y. with two passage tickets in my pocket, and $100 in gold and silver, a letter of credit on a house in San Francisco for $150, and a very fair outfit consisting of clothes, arms, etc. etc. I have no fear but what I shall reach Cal. without accident, and do well after I arrive their.

This is about the time of the year for the rainy season to set in on the Isthmus. Still I anticipate a pleasant trip going across.

We have about 250 passengers, and they agree together very well, most of them steady young men. One of our firemen came very near dying from drinking ice water, but medical aid promptly administered brought relief. When I first came aboard, I thought the Steerage fare and accomodations rather hard,[13] but not being troubled with sea sickness and enjoying a very fine appetite, I have got along very well. I have been requested to join several parties and partake of their hospitality in crossing the Isthmus, and one party have offered to board me at Panama, provided we are detained their, for .37 ½ per day. I shall send this letter from Panama, and will close until I reach their.

Panama 19th July 1849

I arrived here in good health on Sunday 15th inst. and expected to send this to you by "Crescent City," but found that her mail had closed when I arrived here and shall send this per "Falcon."[14] We arrived at mouth of Chagres River on morning of 9th inst., but the anchorage being bad the "C.C." went to Limon Bay 6 miles from Chagres. In the afternoon a small steamer called "Orus."[15] came along side and the baggage was put on board, but we did not leave for Chagres untill morning of the 10th inst., when we were landed on the American side of the River in a hard shower.[16] Previous to leaving the ship I had connected myself with a party of 3 gentlemen, (one of whom spoke Spanish very fluently, which is the language of this country) for the purpose of crossing the Isthmus in company. It is customary for the "Orus" to take passengers up the River as far as she can go and then furnish them with Canoes to take them to either Gorgona or Cruses [Cruces]. But in consequence of not be-

Like other 49ers who crossed the Isthmus of Panama, Churchill traveled two-thirds of the way in a dugout which was poled up the Chagres River. "Incident on the Chagres River," painted in 1867 by Charles Christian Nahl.

ing able to hire the canoes, we were obliged to hire our own
canoes and make the whole journey in them, with every
prospect of being three or four days on the river in the very
worst kind of weather. The American town as it is called
consists of three or four board shanties, called hotels. I
crossed the river to see the town itself. It contained about 400
inhabitants and such a medley population I never saw. The
Negro and Indian seemed to predominate; occasionally a
pure blood white man was to be seen. They seem to mix
colors and races in a way that was quite astonishing to me.
A white man will take an Indian woman, or even a Negro,
for his wife. The houses are built of bamboo or cane and covered with straw or palm leaves. After some trouble we engage[d] a passage in a whale boat manned by 4 natives—
to Cruses for [14?] each. We paid half down and after waiting until they had spent their money in Chagres we started
up the river.[17] The river is about 100 yards wide, but in the
rainy season their is plenty of water in the channel for large
Steamboats and the current is very swift. Our progress therefore was very slow.[18] At one o'clock in the morning we
reached an Indian village called Gatuna [Gatun] 9 miles
from Chagres. The village contains about 800 souls. We
found plenty of bad coffee but nothing to eat. Fortunately
we had provided ourselves with provisions. Some of our
party slept in the boat, others slept on mats spread on the
ground in the huts. At 10 o'clock we left Gatuna but had to
use forcible measures with one of our natives as he insisted
on spending the day in the village. We travelled 11 miles
and at night stopped at a miserable ranch. As it was not raining I spread my blankets on the ground and obtained a few
hours sleep. We travelled in the night as much as possible to

avoid the heat. At 2 o'clock in the morning we got under way. At 11 o'clock we stopped to breakfast and allow our men a few hours rest. At dark we reached an Indian village and as it was raining we had hoped to obtain a mat in some of the huts, but so many canoes were in advance of us that all the accomodations were engaged. So we spread our blankets on top of our baggage in our boat and composed ourselves to sleep in defiance of the rain. We got under way about 3 o'clock in the morning, and when we started I woke up wet through with the rain, and chilled with the cold. Fortunately we had some whiskey and a big drink of it soon produced a sweat, otherwise I certainly would have been sick. By urging our boatmen we reached Gorgona by the middle of the afternoon. It is said to contain 800 inhabitants, and the people and houses very much resemble those of Chagres. In consequence of the river being very high we decided not to proceede to Cruses distant 8 miles from Gorgona. Gorgona is about 55 miles from Chagres, and 22 from Panama. Cruses, in consequence of a bend in the River, is about the same distance from Panama.[19] My recollections of Gorgona are not very pleasant as it rained all of the time while I was their. The next morning (Saturday 14th inst.) we placed our baggage in the hands of the Alcalde to be transported to Panama, for which we paid $6., per 100 lbs. The Alcalde at Gorgona is said to be a responsible man and he *generally* sends baggage through safe. Mine reached here yesterday and greatly rejoiced I was to see it, but the rest of my party have not received theirs. I would recommende to persons crossing the Isthmus, to never trust their baggage out of their sight, no matter how responsible the party might be. I had made up my mind to walk from Gorgona, but I heard such bad accounts of the roads that I was afraid to attempt it. The horses here are very small, not more than half the size of our horses.[20] Our party started about 10 o'clock and we had some hopes of reaching Panama the same day, but we soon gave that up. The roads were so wretched muddy that we were glad to take two days to the trip. My horse was stuck in the mud several times with nothing but his head and tail in sight. I had to dismount and get him out the best way I could. We travelled 12 miles and night coming on stopped at a hut, wet and hungry. One of my party had lost his horse in the mud. We could get nothing to eat, but by paying .25c were allowed to sleep on the ground floor under the hut, and $12\frac{1}{2}$c more produced a cup of a vile mixture called coffee. We made an early start in the morning and reached this place about noon, but my horse gave out 2 miles from here. Neither coaxing or beating would induce him to move. Immediately on arrival I hired a room in company with one of my party. We pay $1. each per week, and by economy can live for $1. per day. The steamer in which I will sail is here (the Panama) and will leave for San Francisco about first August. A Danish barque sailed on 16th inst., and two vessels are here now waiting for passengers. One will probably sail in a few days. At present their is no difficulty in obtaining a passage to California in sailing vessels, price of passage $125—Steerage, and $175—Cabin. Steamer tickets are in demand and I could sell mine at a profit if was so disposed.[21]

This is one of the oldest places on the continent, everything bears the appearance of age. It contains about 8,000 inhabitants. It has been built up and worn out.[22] It has been a Saint's week since I have been here, and such a terrible clatter of bells I never heard. They put three or four in a steeple and ring them all at once, and have a fife and drum in front of the church, to help out the harmony. The show winds up by firing two or three canons. The accounts from California still continue favorable. One man who was a passenger in "C.C." died of cholera at Cruses. There were a few cases of cholera in the place. My health has been excellent, never better.

21st. The Steamer Oregon[23] arrived today from San Francisco. I am somewhat tired and homesick, anxious to be on my way to California. The weather is warmer here now than what you have in Ohio during the summer, but the great difficulty is the heat continues without intermission.

24th. I have an opportunity to send this by private hand, per steamer "Empire City"[24] and shall avail myself of it. I expect to leave here on the 28th inst., in "Panama,"[25] and will be in San Francisco about 20th Aug. My health is excellent, I hope you are all equally blest. You will of course inform Barton of how I am getting along. You had better send this to him after you have read it. I trust that Mother is boarding with him. I have not time to say more. You will hear from me as soon as I reach San Francisco. I do not expect to go to the mines but to remain in San Francisco.

Your Brother,
C. W. Churchill

No. 2d [Apparently noted by Mendal Churchill]

San Francisco 27th Aug. 49

My Dear Brother

I wrote you from Panama per "Empire City" which I trust was duly received. I reached here on 18th inst. from Panama which place I left on 29th July.[26] The trip from Panama was not very pleasant, the vessel was crowded, the births hot and uncomfortable, and as for eating, salt pork and beef and hard bread was put out in wooden bibs around the hatchway three times a day and each one helped himself. Twice a day we marched up to the galley and got our rations of Tea & Coffee—we had to supply our own plates etc.[27] We reached our first stopping place, Acapulco, 1,500 miles from Panama in the night. The town is on a small bay entirely surrounded by hills. In consequence of the Cholera being at Panama we were not allowed to hold any communication with the shore, altho the captain succeeded in landing the mails before our arrival became known to the authorities.[28] San Blas, our next stopping place is 400 miles from Acapulco. I went ashore to see the town but think I was scarcely paid for my trouble and expense. It owes most of its importance to its being the seaport of Tepeic [Tepic] which is some 40 miles inland.[29] Mazatlan our next port we had no opportunity to go ashore.[30] We reached San Diego the first Amn. port in Cal. on 14th inst. We only saw the landing. The town itself is some 3 miles up a small bay.[31] Monterey we arrived at on morning of 18th inst. I like the situation of the town better than this place at which we arrived late in the afternoon of the same day. . . . [this letter is continued in the next chapter].

34

NOTES

1. Charles E. Rosenberg, *The Cholera Years: The United States in 1832, 1849, and 1866* (Chicago: University of Chicago Press, 1962), pp. 114-15.

2. Bayard Taylor, *Eldorado, or Adventures in the Path of Empire* (New York: Alfred A. Knopf, 1949), p. 3. Taylor left New York on June 28; Churchill left on June 30.

3. John Haskell Kemble, *The Panama Route, 1848-1869* (Berkeley: University of California Press, 1943), pp. 147-148.

4. Kemble, *Panama Route*, p. 36.

5. "My Journey to the Gold Fields. Reminiscences of An Argonaut," *The American West*, XIII, 3 (May-June, 1976), 5.

6. Cholera, according to one Dr. Byrd of Chicago, resulted from a deficiency of ozone in the atmosphere. Byrd prescribed sulphur pills to counteract the ozone shortage and his worthless remedy spread across the country along with cholera in 1849. Although useless, sulphur was less extreme than tobacco-smoke enemas, strychnine, or electric shocks, which members of the American medical profession also prescribed. See Rosenberg, *The Cholera Years*, p. 152.

7. Betsey, Melissa, and Julia were Churchill's three sisters. See brief outline of the Churchill family in the appendix. Barton, whom Charles mentions frequently in his early correspondence, was apparently Henry Barton, a local merchant who had loaned money to his mother and for whom Mendal worked.

8. Apparently the mother of Charles' brother-in-law, Elisha B. Greene.

9. Eddy may have been the five-year-old son of Charles' sister and her husband, Joseph Franklin Wheeler.

10. Probably a relative of Joseph Wheeler, the husband of Charles' sister Melissa.

11. A wooden side-wheel steamer of 1,291 tons, with two decks and three masts. Built in 1847-1848, the *Crescent City* made its first New York-Chagres run from December 23, 1848 to January 2, 1849, for J. Howard and Son. By early 1849 the ship was largely owned by Charles Morgan. During the first six months of 1849, until Morgan put the Empire City into service, the *Crescent City* was the only steam vessel to compete for passenger service to Chagres with the U.S. Mail and Steamship Company.

12. At first, steerage fare from Panama to San Francisco was $100 (compared to $250 for first cabin). By July the Pacific Mail Steamship Company had raised its price to $150 for steerage. Many paid more, however, for heavy demand encouraged a brisk business in scalping tickets. Steerage was cramped and crowded, with each passenger entitled to a berth six feet long and one and a half feet wide.

13. Accommodations and food on the Pacific side were even "harder," as Churchill would soon discover. Daniel Knower, who sailed on the *Crescent City* with Churchill, described the voyage thus: "Our course was to the east of

35

Cuba. We passed in sight of the green hills of San Domingo to our left, and the sight of Jamaica to our right, crossing the Caribbean sea, whose grand gorgeous sunsets I shall never forget." *The Adventures of a Forty-Niner,* edited by Kenneth M. Johnson (Ashland, Oregon: Lewis Osborne, 1971), p. 23.

14. Beginning in December 1848, the *Falcon,* a wooden side-wheel steamer, became the first vessel to make regular runs between New York and Chagres for the United States Mail Steamship Company.

15. The *Orus,* a wooden, side-wheel steamer built in 1842, had been sent from New York to Chagres with passengers in December 1848. She was to serve on the Chagres River between Chagres and Gorgona or Cruces, but since she was too large to go more than fifteen or twenty miles up the river, passengers made the remainder of the journey in native dugouts. Churchill was not so fortunate and had to use native craft all the way from Chagres to Gorgona. Late in 1849 the *Orus* was purchased by Cornelius Vanderbilt for service on the San Juan River in Nicaragua.

16. The village of Chagres was located on the left bank of the river of the same name. With the growth of traffic across the Isthmus a town, consisting mainly of hotels and saloons for travelers, had grown up across the river and was known as the "American town."

17. The rate had been $10 at first, but it rose to what the traffic would bear, some people reporting payments as high as $40 or $50. It was customary to pay half down and the remainder upon completion of the trip.

18. Perhaps the rainy weather blinded Churchill to the beautiful and extraordinary tropical scenery, about which he makes no comment. Other travelers, such as Bayard Taylor, who sailed up the Chagres at the same time that Churchill did, exclaimed about "all the gorgeous growths in an eternal summer . . . so mingled in one impenetrable mass that the eye is bewildered. . . . Every turn of the stream only discloses another and more magnificent vista of leaf, bough, and blossom" (*Eldorado,* p. 13).

19. Gorgona is thirty-nine and a half miles from Chagres and twenty miles from Panama City. Cruces was two miles closer to Panama. During the dry season, from December to April, travelers usually stopped at Gorgona because the river became too shallow to proceed to the shorter Cruces road. Stopping at Gorgona, Churchill was forced to take the unpaved Gorgona trail to Panama City. That trail turned into a quagmire in the rainy season (May-November).

20. Other travelers, too, noted that horses were small. J. Ross Browne described them as "tough little mustangs, which I could almost step over" (*Eldorado,* p. 19). Most Isthmian travelers, however, hired mules instead of horses.

21. Bayard Taylor, in Panama City at the same time as Churchill, reported 700 persons waiting for passage. "All the tickets the steamer could possibly receive had been issued and so great was the anxiety to get on, that double

price, $600 [first cabin], was frequently paid for a ticket to San Francisco" (*Eldorado*, p. 24). According to Daniel Knower, a lottery was held for sixty tickets on the steamer Panama. Travelers like Knower, who did not have the good fortune to hold a ticket, made a mad dash across the Isthmus and spent many anxious moments waiting for a ship with space.

22. Panama was nearly two centuries old in 1849, with impressive public buildings and paved streets. Taylor thought it "one of the most picturesque cities on the American continent" (*Eldorado*, p. 23). Churchill's estimate of the city's population was sound.

23. Built for the Pacific Mail Steamship Company, this wooden side-wheel steamer sailed from New York on December 8, 1848, reaching San Francisco on April 1, 1849. It was the second vessel put into service by Pacific Mail, having been preceded to Panama by the *California*. Churchill seems unaware that the *Oregon* had injured her keel on the run from San Francisco. By the time he shipped out of Panama City on July 29, the *Oregon* was beached and undergoing repairs, according to Bayard Taylor.

24. On July 17, 1848, the luxurious *Empire City* left New York for Chagres on its maiden voyage, sailing for Charles Morgan and the Empire City Line which also owned the *Crescent City* that brought Churchill to Chagres.

25. A wooden side-wheel steamer built in New York for the Pacific Mail Steamship Company, the *Panama* sailed from New York for San Francisco on February 15, 1849, arriving June 4. It sailed south for Panama again on June 20, continuing regular service between the two cities until 1853.

26. Churchill provides us with a laconic description of his voyage on the *Panama*. Bayard Taylor, a journalist who was on the ship with Churchill, provides a fuller description in chapters four and five of his *Eldorado*.

27. Steerage passengers on the overcrowded steamers on the Pacific in 1849 had to furnish their own eating utensils, plates, and bedding, and ate inferior food. First- and second-cabin passengers fared better, but they too fought with one another for food at their tables, leading Bayard Taylor to comment: "I never witnessed so many disgusting exhibitions of the lowest passions of humanity as during the voyage" (*Eldorado*, p. 27).

28. The captain hoped to land to take thirty or forty Americans aboard, but was warned that if the ship landed it would be fired upon. See Taylor, *Eldorado*, p. 29 and Knower, *Adventures of a Forty-Niner*, pp. 33-34.

29. Some 500 international nautical miles from Acapulco, San Blas had been founded in 1767 as a supply base for exploration and expansion along the Pacific coast. The original Spanish presidio was abandoned by 1849. The new town, which languished until the gold rush, was located in a tropical jungle made memorable by unmerciful mosquitos. Travelers who had a choice preferred to stay in the mountains at Tepic, about 50 miles distant.

30. Whereas Churchill found Tepic and Mazatlán uninteresting, Bayard Taylor seemed fascinated by both places. Regarding Mazatlán, Taylor wrote,

"few ports present a more picturesque appearance from the sea." He admired "the white walls of Mazatlán, rising gradually from the water, with a beautiful background of dim blue mountains. The sky was of a dazzling purity" (*Eldorado*, p. 33).

31. The *Panama* dropped anchor in front of the hide houses and the landing on Point Loma. Bayard Taylor pronounced San Diego's harbor "the finest on the Pacific with the exception of Acapulco." The *Panama* picked up about fifty passengers at San Diego, including "the first of the overland emigrants by the Gila route, who had reached San Diego a few days before" (*Eldorado*, p. 37). Churchill makes no note of this, but two years later he would follow the Gila River route himself, traveling east into Arizona.

III

THE FORTY-NINER MINER

1849-1850

"A good business provided you are successful"

Then, ho! Brothers ho!
To California go.
There's plenty of gold in the world we're told,
On the banks of the Sacramento.

> "Ho! For California,"
> *Book of Words for the Hutchinson Family*

All the mines look hard and dreary,
Everywhere I roam;
Oh, miners how my heart grows weary,
Ne'er a cent, and far away from home!

> "Away Up on the Yuba,"
> *Original California Songster*

Sluicing near Nevada City, 1852. Daguerreotype reproduced by permission of the California State Library.

CALIFORNIA OF 1849 was unlike anything Charles Churchill, or most other forty-niners, had ever experienced. Perhaps a hundred thousand people rushed to the mother lode
country to tap that promised shortcut to the American
dream. Suddenly it appeared that only a little work would
amply reward the prospector with a wealth of gold that
would open many doors. The pace was fast, high-rolling,
exaggerated, and exciting; Churchill entered into it as en-
thusiastically as any of his fellow forty-niners.

In his letters from August, 1849, through November,
1850, he recounts his fortunes and misfortunes as he pur-
sues that fickle goddess of gold. He landed in San Francisco
during the throes of its first mining boom. A village no
longer, this jumble of jerry-built homes and stores, beached
ships and now, in late 1849, "large and handsome edifices,"
had become the "Queen City" of the new El Dorado. A fortune could be made by those blessed with a combination of
business acumen, ambition, and luck; Churchill, however,
"made up [his] mind to go to the mines," and off he went
to "see the elephant" in all its varied trappings.

Churchill spent most of these months at Mormon Island.
Discovered by Mormons in 1848 on the south fork of the
American River, Mormon Island became nearly as famous
as its neighbor Coloma, the location of Sutter's mill. In 1848
Mormon Island had been overrun, and a "friendly and well

disposed camp" grew like Topsy. By 1849 mining was becoming more work with fewer rewards than in the previous year's balmy days. Hiram Pierce arrived there about three weeks before Churchill landed in San Francisco. He wrote what follows in his diary; though his spelling is quaint, the point is made: "It is verry much like work" (Aug. 6) "The hot Sun & Shining Sands at noon are allmost intolerable. We work from 6 untill betwene 11 & 12 and lay by untill 3 P.M. (Aug. 14). "I felt verry tierd. My back getting lame in consequence as I think of getting my feet wet days & sleeping on the ground nights." (Aug. 22)[1] Churchill, lolling away the restless hours on shipboard, could hardly have imagined what lay ahead for him.

Sacramento, a bustling river port, was the site of Sutter's fort, where John Sutter had made the plans to build the mill that led to the finding of gold in January, 1849, and the collapse of his dream of empire. The trade center for the "northern mines," where Churchill worked, Sacramento was second in importance only to San Francisco.

Churchill concludes this segment of his life at Nevada City, whose potential he sadly misjudged. Nevada City was a young camp in 1850, its mines newly opened. In the 1850s, along with its neighbor Grass Valley, it would become California's most productive quartz mining area. In the course of the more than fourteen months represented by these letters, Churchill toured the old and the new, the prospering and the declining, and the promising mining districts. He saw a large slice of California mining in the search for his personal El Dorado.

No. 2d.
[Apparently noted by Mendal Churchill]

San Francisco 27th Aug. 49

MY DEAR BROTHER

[The beginning of this letter, in which Charles Churchill outlined his voyage from Panama to San Francisco, concluded the previous chapter. Here, we pick Churchill's August 27, 1849, letter up again with his arrival in San Francisco.] . . . we arrived late in the afternoon of the same day [August 18]. The first night I slept on the beach with my baggage, but the next day joined a party who own a tent and have continued with them since. We buy our provisions and do our own cooking and considering that we are in California live very cheap. I delivered my letters of introduction but was soon convinced their was very little hope of my obtaining a situation as clerk. So I made up my mind to go to the mines, but thought it advisable to recruit my finances previous to starting, by working as a day labourer, but so many were in the same situation as myself, that it is not surprising that I could get nothing to do. From what I can learn from those who have just returned from the mines, I can unless I am very unfortunate dig from $8. to $10. per day.

Real estate is enormously high here. Ground rents also. For a small frame store, a very little larger than Barton's Store, in the business part of the city I inquired the price, $800. per month rent, or $9,000 for one year. For a lot 15 x 30 feet on which to erect a tent to sell goods in, $100 per month for the rent of the ground. Goods cannot be purchased at retail except at extravagant prices. A great many are sold at auction and I have seen them sell very cheap. Flour is

$8.50 per bbl. The market is overstocked with tobacco, liquor and common clothing. Fresh meat is 12½c per lb, potatoes 37½c per lb, onions $1.25 per lb, altho at the mines they are worth one dollar each. Very common board without lodging $15. per week. Board and lodging at a good hotel $40. per week. Carpenters and cooks can get from $200. to $300. per month. A number of the hotels and stores are made of canvass, what they will do when the rainy season sets in which will be about first November is more than I can tell. Great quantities of goods are lying in the street which must be stored when the rain commences. San Francisco will be crowded with people next winter and they cannot live in tents as they now do. The climate here is very disagreeable although August, woolen clothing is quite comfortable, and 2 or 3 blankets at night seem indespensible. About 12 m. a cold North west wind sets in. I expected to see plenty of gambling but it far exceeds my expectations. Lumber is $350. per thousand feet. Brick is $300. per thousand.[2]

28th I am making arrangements to start for the mines today. Shall go to Sacramento City and I think from there to Mormon Island. I have been offered $200 per month and found to work for a man at the mines, but have decided not to accept it, altho perhaps I may after I arrive at the mines. I am going in company with a young man, who has travelled with me from New York. The mines which I intend going to are perfectly healthy. Direct to me at San Francisco, it may be sometime before you hear from me again as the communication between here and the mines per letter is very uncertain. I trust that you are all well. I am some distance from home seeking my fortune and hope it may all turn out for the best.

My Love to all   *Your Brother*
                                        C. W. CHURCHILL

No. 3
Rec'd April 5/50
[Apparently noted by Mendal Churchill]

Mormon Island 2d Dec. 1849

Mr. Wm. Churchill Jr.
My Dear Cousin

I wrote you from San Francisco in August. Since I have
been here I have not received a letter from the States, altho
I doubt not their are some at San Francisco for me. I have
sent to the Post Office several times, but expect I will get no
letters untill next spring when I shall go myself. I presume
you are anxious to know how I have succeeded in mining.
In a word then I have not been very fortunate. I left San
Francisco a few days after the date of my letter—for
Sacramento City, on the Sacramento River, distant 130
miles. From Sacramento I walked here a distance of 20
miles and paid 10 cents per lb freight on my baggage consisting of a tent, cooking utensils, and change of clothing.
Before leaving San Francisco I had connected myself with a
young man named Horrell. My first impression of the
mines was not very favorable when I saw the immense
heaps of stones and dirt which had been thrown up in
search for gold. Mormon Island is on the South Fork, and
contains between 6 and 7 acres. It is generally overflown in
the spring. The gold is found within about a foot of the granite, but the granite is from 5 to 15 feet from the top, and it
is considerable work to throw the bank off, altho their will
certainly be some gold found, perhaps not enough to pay.
The Island was nearly all worked over before I arrived here
but the diggings extend 4 or 5 miles down the river and as
far up the river as you choose to go and were very fair last

45

spring, but everything in this vicinity has been well worked over. The gold found here is in small thin scales, and very light. It is deposited along the banks, on the bars, and among the rocks, in the spring when the river is high, and probably comes from the mountains and ravines near where the river takes its rise. My partner and I on our arrival here opened a hole on the Island, but remained there but a few days as we found we could make but 2 or 3 dollars each a day, and have since then worked in different spots along the river, altho our tent has stood at the Island ever since we have been here. There is quite a little settlement of tents here, with occasionally a log house, and 3 or 4 stores. We do our own cooking and washing. During the summer pork was selling here at .50 per lb., flour .25 per lb., sugar .30 per lb. etc.[3]

About middle of October we had made between $200 and $300 each and began to think about going to some dry diggings to spend the winter. I met an old acquaintance here from Buffalo and we made up a party of six and sent two of the party to select a suitable location and one to San Francisco to purchase provisions. Our prospecting party returned with bad accounts. They found Dry Diggings[4] and Ravines where gold was plenty and as long as they lasted a man could make from an ounce to $20 a day, but miners were crowding in by the hundred, and there was no certainty of finding over a few weeks work, and the expense of moving there would be considerable etc. Finally the party broke up, two returned to the states, and two went to San Francisco to winter. My partner and I remained here. It proved an expensive affair to all of us. I then started up the river myself prospecting. I took a pair of blankets, some raw pork and pilot bread, a shovel and tin pan to wash gold.[5]

Gold hunting or "prospecting" as it is universally termed, is very tiresome work and I was absent only 3 days. Returned satisfied to remain here. There are several small dry ravines in this vicinity and we commenced to work in one of them. We had to back our dirt an ⅛ of a mile over a high hill to the river, and by working very hard, could make $10. each per day. My partner thought it was very hard work, and kept at me untill I consented to his purchasing a hole for $50. in a big sand bank, with 25 feet of sand to shovel off, and then to go down 4 foot below the level of the river when we would come to the granite. No gold of any consequence would be found untill we came within 6[?] inches of granite, when it would pay about $50. to a bushell of dirt. Soon after we bought our hole we had about 2 weeks steady rain, and the river which seldom rises any of consequence untill about Feb rose some 3 feet. However we were determined to work our hole out. After spending something over $200. and doing a great deal of work, and when 3 days more of pleasant weather would have enabled us to have worked it out, and received pay for all our labour done and money spent, the river commenced to rise very rapidly probaly [probably] owing to heavy rains above, and backed up into our hole, caved the sand down into it, and in short we had all our work to do over again. My partner was taken sick and it required 4 to work the hole properly, and I could not get hands for less than $12 a day as the work is very hard and obliged to be in the water considerable of the time. So I determined to let the hole go, and have been working in a ravine, pitching up the dirt on to the bank waiting for a few days rain to wash it. I have dirt dug that will pay me about $150. when washed. My partner in consequence of sickness suddenly determined to leave the mines, and will start for San Francisco tomorrow morning. I have been busy all day arranging matters with him etc., and have devoted part of the night to writing this letter to you. You may think it strange that I do not remit a little dust to you. Nothing would afford me greater pleasure than to pay Mr Mumford and send something to Mother, but at present I do not feel able. Last winter it rained every day for over 2 months and such may be the case this winter. When the rains have fairly set in, provisions are very high — pork $1. per lb, flour .75 per lb, meal do [ditto], sugar .75 per lb, potatoes $1. per lb, and other articles in proportion. Blankets are worth from $20 to 2 ounces pr. Boots one ounce to 4 ounces, etc. I doubt not pork and flour will be worth $1.50 per lb before the winter is over. I have a small stock of provisions, and buy whenever I can do so at anything less than the prices above. Next spring it is my intention to go up into the mountains. I think with the experience which I have of mining I can make something. I have been unfortunate so far. I know how I could have made $2000 for the time that I have been here. Since we have had rain hauling has been from $25. to $40. per 100 pounds from Sacramento City—here, and to the Mills 15 miles higher up the river one dollar per pound. The roads are splendid during the dry season, but the worst you ever heard off [of] when the rains commence. Pork is $60. per bbl at Sacramento, flour $40. per bbl. Sacramento I understand has grown to quite a town since I passed through it.

In washing gold a cradle or rocker is used. It much resembles a cradle such as is used to rock babies in. One end is left open for the dirt to pass out—the opposite one has a square box with an iron sive [sieve] in the bottom. In this the dirt is placed, water poured on, and the cradle rocked. In about the middle of the cradle on the bottom is a bar 2 inches high. The motion of the cradle, and pouring water on constantly works the gold to the bottom, and the dirt passes out. It is growing late and I must close my letters. I have a faint hope of being able to get my letters from San F. A day does not pass that I do not think of those that I have left behind. I have not time to write Mendall, altho' I shall do so if I can send the letter to San Francisco. Will you please forward this to him.

Truly Yours,

C. W. CHURCHILL

P.S. I have grown stout and hearty since I have been here. The exercise in the open air agrees with me. But such is not the case with all who come here. Within a stones throw of my tent is the Grave Yard. A week does not pass that some poor fellow is put under ground. I think I shall dig by myself in the future. I have a comfortable tent to which I shall make a chimney and hope to pass the winter comfortably.

No. 4
[Apparently noted by Mendal Churchill]

Mormon Island 14th Feb/50

MY DEAR BROTHER
   Your letter of 25th Nov/49 was duly received, making the *first* and *only* letter which I have received since I have been in Cal. I have repeatedly sent to San Francisco for letters, but it was only a few days since that your letter reached me.[6] Sometime in December I wrote Cousin William and

49

requested him to forward the letter to you which I presume reached you.[7] Since then I have remained here, but now that the rainy season is about over I am making preparation to leave for other diggings, as the diggings about here are entirely worked out. I did not enjoy very good health during the rainy season, being troubled with coughs, colds, and a slight touch of the fever, but now that we have not had rain for some two weeks, and the weather is quite pleasant, I have entirely recovered my health, and am getting quite strong and hearty. I had some dirt pitched up out of a ravine which paid me very well and furnished me with work for a part of the winter, but the price of provisions has made it almost impossible to make much over my living, as it cost me about two dollars per day to live. I have not yet decided what diggings I shall go to, but think it probable that I shall go up either the North or South Fork of the American river. Great numbers of people are constantly arriving at San Francisco, and they generally go to the noted diggings such as the Yuba river, Bear Creek, Deer Creek, etc. Thousands have already gone up the Yuba.[8]

You speak of coming here, I would advise you to relinquish the idea. Every spot in California where gold is to be found will be crowded with people. Many a poor fellow will repent ever having come here, and many a one who has been here for sometime would go home if they had money enough to carry them their.[9] The fortunes are for the few, not for all, and when a steamer arrives with dust, recollect the thousands of miners. *Their is but one route* to this country (that is which a man should ever think of coming) and that is across the Isthmus with a *steamer ticket* for this side in his pocket. Howland and Aspinwall of New York are the

Agents of the line on this side, and I believe tickets can be procured only of them.[10] Taking a sailing vessel at Panama, and being from 50 to 100 days to San Francisco is rather unpleasant. Besides it is impossible for me to say where I will be and you might be here for two or three years and never find me. As your first letter did not reach me it is impossible for me to know what preparations you have made for coming here, etc. etc. Two shirts, two pr pants, etc. is all the baggage a man requires in coming to this country, and it is very foolish of him to encumber himself with arms, etc. for he will have no use for them. A man should have no more baggage than he can carry on his back and walk 25 miles a day with. To come the route which I spoke of (across the Isthmus) by taking the cheapest accomodations, $400 would be all the money a man would *require* and then if he intends to come to the mines he ought to be able to save $50. out of that to pay his expenses after reaching San Francisco. I have thus given you some idea of the expense, and most feasible route, etc. to this country, because you desired it. I do not consider my prospects very flatering. I have made only about $400. since I have been here. I have dug considerable dust but you can buy *nothing* here without paying about twenty times its value. I have not worked much since the rainy season set in (except lately) owing to sickness, etc. and the little money which I have will hardly carry me 50 miles from here, and I intend going at least a 100 if not 150 miles from here. I feel quite confident that I shall make something this season, else I would not remain here but return home. Next fall, provided I conclude to remain here another season, I will remit you funds to pay your passage here and arrange for our meeting at some point, but at present I consider mining too uncertain a business to recommend you to come here. When I leave here which I think will be in a week or ten days I expect to sleep under the shade of a tree and live on pork and hard bread, just the *hardest* life a man can lead."[1] Tell John Kyle if I see Game [?] I shall remember him. I think it probable that he is either at Sacramento City or San Francisco, which places I shall probaly not visit untill next fall. It afforded me the greatest of pleasure to hear from you and learn that you were all well. You can form no idea of the gratification of receiving a letter from home when it contained no *bad* news. I shall probaly not hear from you again untill next fall, unless by chance I should meet with an opportunity to send to San Francisco by someone going down and returning from the mines where I may locate. Then the P.O. their is such a miserable affair it is doubtful whether I would get any letters. I have written in great haste as the person by whom I shall send this to Sacramento City leaves tomorrow morning one day sooner than what I anticipated. Consequently I have been compelled to write after supper, and have not been quite as explicit as I designed to be. When I have decided what diggings I shall go to I will write you again, also Cousin William. With regard to your own prospects, it is impossible for me to advise you at present. I can only say to you, to be energetic and persevering and do the best you can. Next fall I shall either start for home or advise you to come here. Untill then do the best you can. I trust that Mother enjoys good health. I need not tell you to give my love to all. You will hear from me soon again.

Your Aff Brother
C. W. Churchill

To Mr Mendall Churchill

52

No. 5
[Apparently noted by Mendal Churchill]

Sacramento City 2d March/50

Mr. Mendall Churchill
Burlington
Ohio

My Dear Brother

I wrote you some weeks since acknowledging receipt of yours of 28 Nov/49, which I trust will come safely to hand. I arrived here yesterday, and was agreeably disappointed at receiving two letters from you—(July 16th and Sept 9th) and five from Cousin William. I have altered my mind respecting the Diggings, and have determined to go up the Yuba river.

It afforded me great pleasure to hear from you all. I do not know that I can add anything to my letter of Feb respecting your coming to this country. If I could spare the means I would remit enough to you to pay your expenses here, but as it is you will probably have to wait a few months at all events. This is a great country for a young man, altho' I would not advise your coming here (under existing circumstances). If I can make money enough to send you $500 and arrange for a meeting at some point I will do it. If Henry Barton concludes to come here, and you should (by any accident) come with him, you had better come to Sacramento City and drop a letter in the P.O. for me stating what mines you have gone to etc. It is probable that I will be high up the Yuba river, or Feather river. I leave for Yubaville tomorrow morning (at the junction of

Nevada City 7th Nov 1850

Mr Mendall Churchill
        My Dear Brother
                        I wrote you from
Sacramento City—last Feb when I was on my way to the
Yuba river. Since leaving their I have not received a letter
from you—in fact but one letter has reached me & that
was from Cousin Wm announcing the melancholy intelligence
of his Mothers death. I feel now considerable anxiety—
to hear from you, & it would afford me unspeakable
pleasure to know that you were all in the enjoyment
of good health, I trust however such is the case.
After leaving Sacramento I went to Marysville, & from
their to Porters Bar on the North Fork of the Yuba — distant
40 miles. I started from Marysville with my blankets—on
my back leaving my baggage to follow in a wagon, but it
soon commenced raining & I was obliged to sleep out two nights
in no very comfortable plight. I remained at Porters
untill April when I started up the river prospecting
At that time the North Fork of the Yuba was considered
the richest stream in California. Thousands of miners were
hurrying up the river to secure claims to work when the
river fell — for you must bear in mind the water was too
high to admit of much work being done on the bars & it was
not untill June that the river was low enough to be worked
to advantage. I accordingly travelled up to the "Fork," 35
miles from Porters. The diggings about the Forks were known
to be good, but it was a very difficult matter to locate
a claim that would warrant a man in laying by for two
or three months before we would be able to prospect it, &

Letter of Charles William Churchill to Mendal Churchill,
November 7, 1850, from Nevada City, California.

Yuba and Feather rivers).[12] Tell Julia she must not be discouraged and imagine that she will have to teach school always. I trust the company of Mother and Julia will reconcile
Betsey to her new home. I would like to know whether
Franklin ran for Prosecuting Atty or not? and whether he
was elected? I write in a room full of company, therefore
excuse me for not writing at greater length. With Love to
all. I shall write you again by first opportunity.

Aff Yours

C. W. Churchill

P.S. If you see persons coming here tell them across the
Isthmus is the route, with a Steamer Ticket for this side. It
will not answer to trust to purchasing one at Panama—
neither to trust to sailing vessels from Panama, as they may
have a passage of 80 or 90 days.

Nevada City 7th Nov. 1850

Mr. Mendall Churchill

My Dear Brother

I wrote you from Sacramento City last Feb when I was
on my way to the Yuba river. Since leaving their I have not
received a letter from you, in fact but one letter has reached
me and that was from Cousin Wm announcing the melancholy intelligence of his Mother's death. I feel now considerable anxiety to hear from you, and it would afford me
unspeakable pleasure to know that you were all in the enjoyment of good health. I trust however such is the case.
After leaving Sacramento I went to Marysville, and from

their to Fosters Bar[13] on the North Fork of the Yuba, distant 40 miles. I started from Marysville with my blankets on my back leaving my baggage to follow in a wagon, but it soon commenced raining and I was obliged to sleep out two nights in no very comfortable plight. I remained at Foster's untill April when I started up the river prospecting. At that time the North Fork of the Yuba was considered the richest stream in California. Thousands of miners were hurrying up the river to secure claims to work when the river fell, for you must bear in mind the water was too high to admit of much work being done on the bars and it was not untill June that the river was low enough to be worked to advantage. I accordingly travelled up to the "Fork" 35 miles from Foster's. The diggings about the Fork were known to be good, but it was a very difficult matter to locate a claim that would warrant a man in laying by for two or three months before we would be able to prospect it, and ascertain whether it was good for anything. The river about the Forks proved to be very *rich* in *spots.* Finally I located on the South Fork of the North Fork—10 miles from the "Fork." I found gold in the bank and on the bars when I could find one that was not covered with water. I remained their untill the latter part of July when the claim which my partner and I had taken up were worked out. We were on a large bar that paid us from one to two ounces per day when the water allowed us to work which was very seldom, and by throwing out a wing dam promised us a seasons work. The "bed rock" was slate. We found no gold in the gravel on the slate, but the slate was full of creavases, and in the creavases we found the gold. We built our dam but with no very sanguine hopes as the river had been turned in several places in our immediate vicinity, and proved an entire failure, their being no gold in the bed of the stream. And such we found to be the case with our claims when we got the water off them. I started on a prospecting tour but found nothing to suit me untill I reached this place. The only diggings here of any note are the Coyota Diggings.[14] They are from 10 to 100 feet below the surface and are worked by sinking wells or shafts, and then drift from the shaft untill all the gravel is taken out from the face of the bed rock. It is rather dangerous looking to one not accustomed to working under ground. I commenced sinking wells when I reached here and was fortunate enough to find one that would pay me small wages. My partner and I took in two lead miners from Galena[15] as we were not acquainted with this kind of mining. We have the claims drifted out and the gravel on top of the ground, and are anxiously waiting for the rains to commence to wash up. We have also bought some gravel which we design to wash, and laid in our stock of winter provisions and have a comfortable log cabin to live in. The Coyota diggings have been unquestionably the richest diggings in California. Some claims have paid as high as $100,000, and it is not uncommon for a claim to pay $10,000, but at the same time they are the most uncertain. A man might dig wells for six months and never see the color of gold. These diggings will now soon be over with for this season as they cannot be worked after the rain sets in. A great number of men will be employed on them next season, but I think the richest Coyota leads have been worked out.

I do not design remaining here after the spring opens. I think it probable I will go up between the Yuba and Feather Rivers in search of dry diggings. Soon after the rain commences and we have got a part of our gravel washed up, I will remit Cousin Wm 25 ounces of dust, a part of which I shall direct him to forward to you for Mother. I think next spring will bring me out about $1000. ahead of the game. I have enjoyed excellent health. The cholera is at Sacramento City, (80 miles from here) but I have no fear of its coming here.

A "claim" in this country is 30 square feet. Flour is worth here now 20c per lb. Pork 40c—Coffee, Sugar and Beans 50c per lb. When I first went on the Yuba I paid $1.00 per lb for Flour and for Pork, Sugar and Coffee $1.50 per lb.[16] I would have made money their if I could have lived without eating, or had not been compelled to lay idle so long waiting for the river to fall. I have given up the idea of seeing home for two or three years. It is of no use for me to return unless my fortunes are mended. I like the country and a miners life. I have since last spring (untill a few weeks back) slept in a hammock slung between two trees out in the open air.

We have now a P. O. in this place, and if you write soon after the receipt of this please direct to "Nevada City," but as my stay in this place is rather uncertain, when you write a second time you had better direct to San Francisco.

The letter which I made mention of as coming from Cousin Wm was dated 12th April and made no mention of your designing to come to California, therefore I trust that you have made up your mind to remain at home. Mining is a good business provided you are successfull, but if you are unfortunate it is the most discouraging business a man ever followed. However I hope to soon peruse a sheet from you and please give me your views on the subject.

I believe a majority [of] those who came through this season will return home as soon as they can make money enough to carry them their, and a large part of them will barely be able to make their living this winter.

Do not delay writing. You will hear from me again soon. I sincerely hope you are all in the enjoyment of good health. I feel particularly anxious about Mother. With Love to all.

Your Aff Brother
C. W. Churchill

NOTES

1. Hiram Pierce, *A Forty-Niner Speaks* (Oakland: Keystone-Inglett Printing Co., 1930), pp. 34-36. J. M. Letts, in his *California Illustrated* (New York: R. T. Young, 1853), tells of his Mormon Island adventures, particularly emphasizing his experiences with the Mormons and his near misses at finding wealth.

2. Churchill was not alone in his amazement over the high prices in California during the early gold rush years. William Gill wrote his wife in November, 1850, from Grass Valley, that there were plenty of provisions, "but everything is very high you will think." Writing in his *Mining in the Pacific States* (1861), John Hittell concluded that the cost of living in the California mines was about twice as much as in the Eastern states.

3. Nearly a year later, Gill's prices in Grass Valley were very similar. For example, flour was selling at 25c a pound, pork at 40c, and sugar at 50c. Other prices were: corn meal, 25c; potatoes, 30c; coffee, 50c; and dried fruit, 45c a pound.

4. Dry diggings were those that held no natural water supply, except in the wettest season of the year. The yield during the late winter months was often large, but the period of working short. See Rodman Paul, *California Gold* (Cambridge, Mass: Harvard University Press, 1947).

5. Churchill's outfit was typical. "Pilot Bread" might refer to hardtack or ship's bread; more likely it was the miner's own baked bread, some form of quick bread, leavened with saleratus or baking soda. Bread was the staff of life for the miner, or, as the Scotsman J. D. Borthwick said, the bread was very solid and heavy, a little went a long way, "which of itself is no small recommendation when one eats only to live." The pan was the miner's all purpose tool. Leonard Kip, who spent some time in the Mokelumne mines in 1849, pointed out that it was not an uncommon thing to see the same pan used for washing gold and clothes, mixing flour cakes, and feeding the mule. The miner had to avoid getting it greasy, however, for that affected its use in gold panning.

6. Churchill's complaint about not receiving mail was echoed by numerous 49'ers. The miners were hungry for news from home, letters being their main source. *"Letters from home!* If anyone would learn the full significance of these words, let him pass ten months in California without one word from his loved ones, an unhappy exile from his own family," lamented Daniel Woods, who mined in some of the same areas as did Churchill.

7. Churchill refers to his letter of December 2, 1849, which precedes the present letter in this volume. Mendal received and saved that letter.

8. It was on the south fork of the American River in January, 1848, that James Marshall found the gold which started the California rush. The forks of the American River were the scene of large-scale operations in the 1850s, with dams, canals, and flumes diverting and storing water as the river bed was attacked. The Yuba River was likewise the site of much excitement. Nevada City was known early as Deer Creek; perhaps Churchill referred to this area. He would go there eventually.

9. Contemporary Thomas Kinkade agreed, as did others: "This much however I am constrained to say, through charity, to Brethren in the States. Stay at home—stay at home." He also thought the "country is filled to overflowing long ago."

10. Gardiner G. Howland and William Henry Aspinwall, whose international trading firm held controlling interest in the Pacific Mail Steamship Company.

11. Speaking of the miner's life, Louise Clappe, in her famous *Shirley Letters*, observed, "Really, everybody ought to go to the mines, just to see how little it takes to make people comfortable in the world."

12. Marysville, where the Yuba River joined the Feather River, was first called Yubaville. Established at the end of 1849, Marysville was at the head of navigation on the Feather, the main tributary of the Sacramento. The Yuba was the site of some rich discoveries in 1848-49, and the Feather was famous as early as 1848. Along this stream one man with a gang of Indians collected 273 pounds of gold. At Parks Bar, five men took out 525 lbs. of gold within a few days and wisely gave up mining to return home.

13. Foster's Bar, opened in late 1848, was reported to have about 1,000 people.

14. Short shafts sunk into hillsides until they struck paydirt. Popular usage termed them "coyote holes." See Paul, *California Gold*.

15. Galena, Illinois was the famous lead mining district in the 1840s. Mining had begun there in the 1820s.

16. By noting the items for which Churchill gives prices, an idea of a miner's diet can be acquired. The irrepressible Dame Shirley noted in January, 1852, that the miners at Indian Bar subsisted on potatoes, onions, "hard, dark hams," dried mackerel, "rusty pork," flour, oysters, preserved meats, and sardines. The last she detested. To this list, John Eagle added beans, dried apples, molasses, sugar, tea, coffee, and "good bread," when telling his children back in Allegheny City, Pennsylvania, what he had to eat.

IV

FROM CALIFORNIA TO SONORA FOR GOLD

1851

"A foolish expedition"

Farewell, Old California, I'm going far away,
Where gold is found more plenty, in larger lumps, they say;

"Australia and the Amazon,"
Original California Songster

Oh, don't you remember the ship-loads that went,
In spite of their friend, Uncle Sam,
With knives, guns and pistols, they started hell-bent,
For greasers they didn't care a damn.

"The Sonora Filibusters,"
Original California Songster

Pima Indians. Churchill's party followed the Gila River to the prosperous and hospitable villages to the northwest of Tucson.

Dame Fortune having eluded him in the gold fields of California, Charles William Churchill headed south in the spring of 1851 to seek his fortune in Sonora, in northwestern Mexico. As Churchill explained it in the two letters which follow, a group of Americans had learned about rich diggings that remained unworked in Sonora because of Indian hostility. In a classic case of the grass looking greener, a group of forty-eight armed Americans started for Sonora, Churchill among them.[1]

It is both curious and ironic that these Americans should go prospecting in Sonora at the same time that thousands of Sonorans were migrating northward to try their luck in the California mines. Apaches and Yaquis had made mining so treacherous for Sonorans that even the United States seemed to offer greater security, although it was inhabited by Anglo-Americans whom one Sonoran termed "natural enemies of our race."[2] In the eight months between October 1848 and May 1849, an estimated five to six thousand persons left Sonora for California.[3] Sonorans continued to emigrate in such large numbers that by 1853 the northern portion of the state was becoming depopulated.[4] The story of the Sonorans' migration to California and the discrimination they met at the hands of Anglo-Americans is well known.[5] Churchill's account of an Anglo-American mining venture in Sonora represents the other side of the coin, the side which has seldom been seen.

Moving against the current of humanity, then, Churchill and his companions made their way south from the gold fields of California to Los Angeles, which they reached in mid-May 1851. On May 17 the *Los Angeles Star* told its readers of a group of prospectors who might have been Churchill's group:

> "A company of men passed through this city on Friday on their way to the Black and Gila rivers, where gold is represented to be very abundant. . . . They are well armed and need fear nothing from any conflict with the Indians. Should they succeed they will undoubtedly be followed by other companies."[6]

From Los Angeles, Churchill and his companions journeyed across the desert to the Colorado River, then picked up the Gila River which they followed into what is today Arizona. In 1851 the Gila formed the northern boundary of Sonora, so when the prospectors headed south from the river to Tucson and Tubac, they were in Sonora. Three years later the Gadsden Purchase would move the boundary farther south and put Tucson and Tubac in the United States.

According to Churchill, Mexican officials viewed the well-armed Americans as an invading force and obstructed their efforts at mining. In hopes of obtaining permission to mine, the Americans sent a four-man delegation to the state capital, Ures. Daniel M. Cook, Hiram B. Bronson, John McDermitt, and Joel Ringo reached Ures by mid-July. On July 18 they petitioned the government on behalf of forty-four other men, whose names they provided.[7] They asked the government to issue them *cartas de seguridad*, or letters of security. Such letters were required for foreigners who desired to travel in the interior of Mexico, and were required in addition to passports. The Americans did not ask for permission to mine, or even mention mining in their petition; perhaps they hoped first to legitimize their presence in the country. If so, the strategy failed. On July 21, Governor José de Aguilar y Escoboza denied their request for letters of safe conduct on the grounds that they had entered the country illegally without passports.[8] Churchill reported that they had received a "conditional permit" to mine. If so, it was probably not put in writing. Instead, as Churchill explained, authorities in Ures soon ordered the Americans to leave the state. The main party probably did not advance deeper into Sonora than Arizpe.[9]

The refusal of Sonora officials to issue letters of safe conduct to the Americans probably had little to do with the niceties of the law regarding passports. Rather, authorities suspected their motives, as an article in a Guadalajara newspaper suggested:

"According to a notice published in the official newspaper of that State [Sonora], there are now sixty-six adventurers, well-armed and provisioned with tools to work the gold placers, who have gathered in that border area hoping for an answer from the government concerning their request for permission to exploit the mines. Local officials have hindered them from insinuating themselves when they do not present their passports. See, then, how our fears are being realized. Before, there were only forty-eight adventurers [Churchill's party]. Today they have nineteen more, and very soon perhaps they will outnumber the forces of those communities [in northern Sonora]."[10]

Mexicans had ample reason to view the well-armed prospectors with suspicion in the summer of 1851. Just a few years earlier the United States had acquired half of Mexico's territory in the so-called Mexican War and some Americans regretted that Sonora, with its fine harbor at Guaymas, had not come with the package. Indeed, in the spring of 1851 California newspapers carried frequent reports of Americans heading to Sonora under various pretexts. One group of Americans in Los Angeles in early May 1851, for example, announced their intention to go to Sonora to obtain land. The *Daily Alta California*, however, noted that "it is perfectly understood, from the preparation of the party, that they intend making a forcible seizure of Sonora."[11] The most notorious of these would-be invaders of Sonora was Joseph C. Morehead, a Kentucky lawyer-turned-army officer, politician, embezzler, and thief, who was recruiting a private army in California in the spring of 1851. By May rumors had reached Sonora that an army of 4,000 was advancing on the state.[12]

Under these circumstances, it is not surprising that Mexicans regarded Churchill and his companions as invaders, or *filibusteros*, and discouraged them from remaining in Sonora. Certainly, the possibility exists that Churchill was an unwitting party to a filibustering attempt, or that he knew that the expedition had ulterior motives, but did not reveal them in his personal correspondence. Either possibility seems unlikely. First, it would have been difficult to conceal the expedition's intentions from its members. Second, Churchill would have had no reason to lie to his relatives had he been part of an invading force; most Americans of his era applauded efforts to "liberate" northern Mexico.

Frustrated by authorities in Mexico and hindered by the scarcity of water, the prospectors from California soon abandoned Sonora. By early autumn they had returned to the California coast. Some of the men came into San Diego in the last week of September. The local paper reported that "They have not been very successful—averaging only about $4.00 each, per day."[13] Three members of the party, apparently including Charles Churchill, reached Los Angeles by October 3 and provided the *Los Angeles Star* with a more detailed account of their misadventures:

> "It will be remembered that in May last a company of forty men passed through this city, on their way to Sonora, in Mexico. Three of them arrived in town yesterday, having been absent about five months. The rest of the party, excepting one who has died, are on their way hither, and may be expected daily. Their object has been to explore the country and prospect for gold. They state that they found gold, silver, and cinnabar all through the southern part of California, but the gold as a general thing, is not sufficiently abundant to pay for working. On the north side of the Gila they found a very rich silver mine, where they stopped about six weeks. While there, a large party of Mexicans arrived from Sonora, but the Indians forced them to leave. In Sonora they went as far as the town of Altar, about 300 miles from the boundary line. In the north-

ern part they found silver and gold, but the expense of transporting provisions to the mines, and the scarcity of water prevents their being worked with profit.

The men state that they were courteously treated in every town through which they passed. The authorities would not grant them permission to mine, but told them they were at liberty to "prospect" as much as they pleased.

The country of Sonora they represent is in many places destitute of vegetation, and uninviting in every respect. Water is very scarce. In coming up they were two days and nights without water.

At some places the Mexicans mistook them for Morehead and his party, regarding whose contemplated expedition they had heard.[14]

Charles Churchill seems to have been one of the three men who arrived in Los Angeles on October 3 in advance of the rest of the party, because on that day he wrote a letter from Los Angeles to his cousin William in New York, briefly outlining his journey. William Churchill received that letter toward the end of November and sent it on to Mendal Churchill with the observation that Charles "appears to have acted with little judgment in moving about so much."[15] Charles Churchill's brief letter of October 3 to William Churchill follows, as does a fuller accounting of his Sonoran adventure in a letter of January 20, 1852, written to Mendal.

Los Angeles 3d Oct 1851

Mr. Wm Churchill Jr

MY DEAR COUSIN

I wrote you from this place last May when I was on my way to Sonora. I have return[ed] this far on my road to the upper country and regret to be compelled to tell you the trip proved an entire failure. The distance was much fa[r]ther than what we anticipated when we started, and we had to encounter hardships that we never dreamed of. We have been about 700 miles from here. We travelled 225 miles up the Rio Gila, but did not prospect any on that stream. The principal cause of the entire failure of our expedition was the extreme dryness of Sonora. The season had been unusually dry and we could prospect but little owing to the scarcity of water. Also the Sonorian gouverment was afraid of us and refused to permit us to remain in the country or allow us to mine, but they were not able to drive us out. We cared very little about the gouvernment futher[other?] than they would not allow any of the natives to act as guides for us to show us the country etc. We found gold, but not as abundant as California. In returning, a great number of the men were sick with the "chills and fever." I was unfortunate enough to have them, but have got rid of them now and think they will not trouble me any more. With regard to my prospects I have spent all my money and shall go into the mines as poor as I was when I first landed in California. Still I feel quite cheerful about it and still hope to make something in California. I shall probably stop in the southern mines and as soon as I am located will not fail to send

71

you my address as I am very anxious to hear from you and from Ohio. I will also give you a more full account of my trip to Sonora in search of gold, and hope it may interest you some, altho' it proved a hard journey to me in several ways. Please forward this to Mendall when you have read it. Hoping that you all enjoy good health. With love to all

Truly Yours etc
C. W. CHURCHILL

DEAR BROTHER

You will also hear from me as soon as I am located, with love to all

Truly Yours etc
C. W. C.

Mariposa Co Cal 20th Jany 52

Mr Mendall Churchill

MY DEAR BROTHER

I wrote cousin Wm sometime since from Los Angeles and requested him to inform you of my return to California from Mexico. I intended long ere this to have written you myself, but I have been in what the miners call a "streak of very bad luck," since I returned from the lower country, and delayed writing you by hoping to be able to inform you that I got into some good diggings. Besides I was uncertain whether I would remain in this section of the country. I have consumed most of my time in travelling around from one mining district to another. I have however settled down for the winter, with only the prospect of making from three to five dollars per day. A dull show when you consider the expense of living in Cal and the bad weather when nothing can be made. I am now near Mariposa River in the extreme southern mines. They have been but little worked in comparissen to the northern mines, which is their only recommendation, for they are infinitely poorer. I think the working men of this section of the country do not average over two dollars per day. It is true occasionally rich diggings are struck, but very rarely. I consider the only chance I have left to make money in California will be by draining the San Joaquin next summer. Very little is known about the river but it is supposed to be rich in the bed of the stream. I shall risk it next summer and it is the only thing which keeps me in this part of the country. Now with regard to my prospecting trip to Sonora, I feel ashamed of myself for ever going on such a foolish expedition.

The party was raised in this way. A Mexican stated previous to his coming to California he was driven out of ravine diggings in Sonora that payed from six to eight ounces per day, by Apache Indians, which were known to be very bad in the northern part of Mexico. He told his tale with such an air of candour and truthfulness that it was generally believed. He also offered to accompany the party and act as guide, provided that he was allowed to work in the diggings. A party was secretly organized to visit the rich diggings, and it was my misfortune to be admitted in the party. Before we started the Mexican struck a rich Quartz lead, and not being able to dispose of it to advantage, the party proceeded without him (a very great mistake). Our party numbered 47,[16] all well armed and mounted with a good train of pack mules. The journey was quite pleasant untill we reached Los Angeles 500 miles south of Stockton.[17]

The country from Stockton to Los Angeles is mostly covered with large ranches. These ranches are covered with horses and cattle (but cattle principally). It is nothing to see 10 or 15000 head of cattle on a ranch. The market for these cattle is of course the mines. Very little cultivation is carried on, a few acres for a garden suffices for a ranch that contains thousands of cattle. Breeding stock is their business. Most of these ranches are owned by native Californian's, altho' a few of the best are owned by Americans, and are held by a mexican grant made before California belonged to the U.S. A large portion of the land is susceptible of cultivation by irrigation. From Los Angeles to the crossing of the Colorado River is 275 miles. 130 miles of it is what is called a desert for in certain seasons of the year their is neither feed for animals nor water, but at the time we crossed their was water in two places in large lagoon's left their by the overflow of the Colorado. We crossed the Colorado two miles below where the Gila empties into it. The river is not as large as the Ohio. We travelled up the Gila River on the south side to Peno's [Pima's] Village 225 miles.[18]

You must bear in mind their are no Mexican settlements on the lower part of the Gila and Colorado River's. The Peno's and Maricopas (who live adjoining to the Peno's) cultivate considerable land by irrigation from the Gila River.

From the Peno's to the frontier town of Tubson [Tucson] is 100 miles without water.[19] We left the river in the afternoon, and was forty hours on the desert without water, excepting the small supply each man carried. You must bear

Tubac. When Churchill visited Tubac in 1851 the town was nearly deserted. Reproduced courtesy of the Arizona State Historical Society Library.

in mind this was in June the warmest month in the year. I thought before that I had suffered for water, but my sufferings were nothing in comparison to what I suffered on that desert. My horse broke down and I was obliged to travel the worst end of the desert on foot. I did not reach water untill I had become entirely speechless. I saw men lay down by the road side to die and their they would have remained had not releif been sent to them. On returning from Sonora I have gone 24 and 36 hours without ever tasting water, and scarcely felt the want of it but then the weather was cool.

We stopped a few days at Tubson to rest ourselves and animals and then proceeded to the deserted town of Tubac (the Apache Indians murdered most of the inhabitants and since then the town has been deserted).[20] We remained there for sometime and also prospected that section of country and endeavoured to obtain Mexican guides as it was rather dangerous to travel much, unless you followed the small water courses, as you might travel for weeks without meeting the water. We could not convince the authorities that we did not intend revolutionary measures, and whenever we entered a small town to purchase provision's etc, the Alcaide [alcalde] beat the drums to quarters and stopped us on the outskirts of the town, telling us that he had positive orders from headquarters not to admit us into town. This was all a farce as far as the Alcaide was concerned, for they dare not molest us, we were too well armed. Besides we always behaved ourselves, but paid no attention to orders, and entered the towns when we felt so disposed. But they prevented our obtaining guides, by forbidding the Mexican's to enter our camp etc. We met with so much opposition from the Mexican authorities that we determined to send a delegation to the capital of the state, Orus [Ures], for a permit to work what mines as we could discover.[21] This consumed some time and they only obtained a conditional permit, but we were all quite surprised after their return to find that the authorities in our vicinity had orders from Orus to drive us out of the country instanter. Their was however no danger of their ever attempting to enforce it. We moved our camp some 40 miles further into the interior of the country, and prospected in the neighbourhood where we supposed the rich diggings to be. There were two or three men in Sonora which we wished to get hold of, who knew where the diggings were we were in search of. But the authorities kept them out of our way. After fruitless endeavours to get hold of the men we wanted as guides, and to find the diggings ourselves, we all became discouraged and voted unanimously to return to California. We found diggings in Sonora that would pay four or five dollars per day during the rainy season, not sufficiently encouraging to remain. These diggings however the mexican's were afraid to work on account of the Apachie's. Numberless town's and large ranches have been deserted in Sonora, in consequence of the residents having been driven out or killed by the Indian's. The inhabitants are not scattered throughout the country as in the "States" but huddled together in small town's, for greater security from the Indian's.

They are mortally afraid of the Apachie's and of truth they have reason to be, for the Indians show them no mercy when they fall into their hands. The Indians when we were at Tubson, came into town, drove out stock, and cut wheat in front of their houses. There is a small garrison their, they beat their drums etc, but never offered to go where the Indians were. They doubtless thought they had the advantage of position where they were. The Indian's never molested us. We were always prepared for every thing that came in our way, either Indian's or Mexican's.

Respecting our return to California I have but little to say. We made the journey quicker returning than going, notwithstanding that our animals were not near as fresh. As for myself I broke down a mule and a horse on the trip. In crossing the desert this side of the Colorado I was siezed with the chills and fever, probably in consequence of drinking bad water. I however got rid of them at Los Angeles. In coming from Los Angeles to the mines we travelled most of the way through the Tulare Valley, said to be one of the finest valleys in the state. No settlements have been made in the valley yet in consequence of the Indians. It lays at the foot of the Sierra Nevada Mountains. A large propo[r]tion of our company crossed the plains to California and they all united in saying our trip to Sonora was harder than the trip across the plains.

I very much fear that my chance for making a "raise" in California is now very small, I have however made up my mind not to quit California as poor as I was when I came here. I have sent to San Francisco with the hope of receiving letters, but was disappointed. I cannot tell you the joy it would give me to see Mother and all of you. You are not often absent from my mind. Write me instanter directed to Mariposa, Mariposa County Cal.

Truly Yours
C. W. CHURCHILL

NOTES

1. The letters which form this chapter appeared in a more lightly edited version of the San Diego Corral of Westerners *Brandbook Four*, ed. by Abraham Nasatir (San Diego: 1976), pp. 23-28, under the title "From California to Sonora For Gold in 1851: The Letters of Charles Churchill," edited by Weber.

2. Manuel Gándara, Governor and Commanding General of Sonora to the Minister of War and Navy, August 12, 1853, in Archivo Histórico de Relaciones Exteriores, doc. no. H/552"853"/1, 6-2-15, Mexico D. F., Mexico.

3 José Francisco Velasco, *Noticias estadisticas del Estado de Sonora* (Mexico: Imprenta de I. Cumplido, 1850), p. 289.

4. Gándara to Minister of War and Navy, August 12, 1853.

5. See, for example, Richard H. Morefield, "Mexicans in the California Mines, 1848-53," *California Historical Quarterly*, 35 (March 1956), 37-46; Leonard Pitt, "The Beginnings of Nativism in California," *Pacific Historical Review*, 30 (February 1961), 23-38; and William Robert Kenny, "Mexican American Conflict on the Mining Frontier, 1848-1852," *Journal of the West*, 6 (October 1967), 582-92.

6. According to his letter of October 3, 1851, to his cousin William, Charles Churchill was in Los Angeles in May 1851.

7. Documents regarding this matter are in the Archivo Histórico del Estado de Sonora, gaveta 11-1, carpetón 223, expediente 2. The list of members of Churchill's party is reproduced in an appendix to this volume. We are grateful to Cynthia Radding de Murrieta of the Instituto Nacional de Antropología e Historia, Centro Regional del Noroeste, Hermosillo, who located these documents for us.

8. The governor cited articles 2 and 3 of the *"Reglamento sobre pasaportes"* of May 1, 1828, and sent a copy of that *reglamento* to the Americans. The law was very explicit in requiring the traveler to present passports or statements indicating one's origin and purpose in coming to Mexico, *before* entering Mexico. A copy of that reglamento is in Manuel Dublán and José María Lozano, *Legislación Mexicana* (Mexico: Imprenta del Comercio, 1876), II, 69-72.

9. Churchill's group was probably the same party of forty-eight Americans reported near Arizpe in July and August, 1851, according to Joseph A. Stout, Jr., *The Liberators: Filibustering Expeditions into Mexico, 1848-1862, and the Last Thrust of Manifest Destiny* (Los Angeles: Westernlore Press, 1973), p. 44. We have been unable to verify Stout's source; his citation seems to be in error.

10. *La Voz de Alianza de Guadalajara*, reprinted in *El siglo diez y nueve* [Mexico], October 24, 1851, reference courtesy of that indefatigable researcher of *filibusteros*, Joe Park at the University of Arizona.

11. San Francisco *Daily Alta California*, May 17, 1851.

12. Stout, *The Liberators*, p. 44.

13. *San Diego Herald*, October 2, 1851. This brief article identified the men as "A portion of the party of about 50 men who left here last spring for newly discovered gold mines in Sonora," and indicated that the men "returned here last week." This article was reprinted in the San Francisco *Daily Alta California*, October 6, 1851.

14. *Los Angeles Star*, October 4, 1851. Reprinted in the *Daily Alta California*, October 13, 1851.

15. New York, November 22, 1851, in the Churchill Letters, Serra Museum, San Diego. We have chosen not to include a transcription of this letter in its entirety.

16. When the party reached Sonora, they turned a list of forty-eight names into the state government at Ures.

17. The distance from Stockton to Los Angeles is about 340 miles.

18. Travelers turned south at the Pima villages at the confluence of the Santa Cruz and Gila rivers. The Pimas, who had villages at other points along the Gila, too, were successful and admired agriculturists who aided travelers along the Gila Trail. J. Ross Browne wrote that if it were not for the Pimas and the Maricopas, "it would now be impossible to travel from Fort Yuma to Tucson." *Adventures in the Apache Country: A Tour through Arizona and Sonora* (New York: Harper & Brothers, 1871), p. 111.

19. From the Pima Villages to Tucson was about 105 miles. Some travelers made this dreadful journey at night to avoid the heat. Churchill's sparse account of his trek from Los Angeles to Tucson might be augmented by the first-hand account such as *Hepah, California! The Journal of Cave Johnson Couts . . . 1848-1849*, edited by Henry J. Dobyns (Tucson: Arizona Pioneers' Historical Society, 1961), or by more general works such as Ferol Egan's *The El Dorado Trail* (New York: McGraw-Hill, 1970), pp. 151-67.

20. Tubac was the site of a Spanish presidio, built about 1752. Travelers in Arizona in the early 1850s agreed with Churchill that it was either abandoned or semi-abandoned.

21. Ures is located on the Sonora River nearly 60 miles northwest of the present capital of Hermosillo. Ures served as the state capital from 1838-1842, and from 1847-1879.

V

THE MINER TURNS MERCHANT

1852-1855

"I have quit mining"

The merchant will not credit you,
The butcher will not trust,
The baker will not sell you bread
Unless you have the dust.
You ask of them to buy "on tick,"
And they will all confess
They'd like to trust you very well
But couldn't stand the press.

"Couldn't Stand the Press,"
Diggers' Song Book

John Chinaman, John Chinaman,
But five short years ago,
I welcomed you from Canton, John—
But wish I hadn't though;

"John Chinaman,"
Original California Songster

Mariposa, California (ca. 1860). The architecture and haphazard arrangement of buildings are typical for a mining camp. Photograph courtesy of Bertha Schroeder.

During the years 1852-55 Churchill lived and worked in the southern mines. In the early days of the gold rush the districts tributary to Sacramento were known as the northern mines and those tributary to Stockton as the southern mines. The southern mines were opened slightly later and were not, on the average, as rich. There were, however, pockets of ore that produced sudden fortunes for the lucky finders and the incentive to continue the search. The gold-bearing deposits diminished as one traveled south, and Churchill was nearing the southern limit at Mariposa. There were quartz mines in the area, including several prominent ones. Eventually some copper mines would be developed in the western portion of the county.

Mariposa, a community of some 500 people and the county seat, was Churchill's residence for over a year. John Hittell, a forty-niner miner and 1850s sojourner in the southern mines, wrote several years later of Mariposa County, "The towns are small; the population in the placers unsteady and irregular in their mode of life; and the county, taken as a whole, is considered one of the most unpleasant parts of the state for the home of a family."[1] Hampered by a continual water problem, the placers were idle much of the year and Hittell concluded that the miners "either go to other counties or spend their time in dissipation."

The water question vexed mining throughout Churchill's

years in Mariposa. In the first issue of the *Mariposa Chronicle*, January 20, 1854, the editors proclaimed, "We shall earnestly advocate the construction of a ditch to bring the water of the Merced river to this mining region." A letter writer who signed himself "a miner without water" could not have agreed more. "For the wants of the requisite supply of water nearly three-fourths of the mining portion of this County lies idle and unappreciated, and some districts scarcely prospected." Churchill's business fortunes rode on this question as surely as the miners'.

Though Churchill did not discuss it, lawlessness existed and the *Mariposa Chronicle*, April 7, 1854, editorially blasted: "We are fast becoming notorious for the many affrays and groundless assaults perpetrated amongst us by the scores of rascals and desperadoes who stalk over the length and breadth of our county, unwhipped and unhung —a disgrace to the land and a mockery of the very name of justice." To make matters worse, Mariposa County was also the site of the Fremont Grant, ownership of which caused a legal dispute and ill feelings between John C. Fremont and miners within the grant's boundaries.

In his 1854-55 letters, Charles Churchill did not detail all of his activities. His letters suggest that he devoted full time to storekeeping, but he continued to involve himself in mining as evidenced by his name on three quartz claim notices filed with the Mariposa County Recorder. He and his partners located two and relocated a third in the spring of 1854. In April, 1855, he served as Inspector of Elections for the Bridgeport precinct. A check of the Mariposa County assessment rolls for 1854 reveals that he owned property valued at $500, on which he paid $12.50 in taxes. Our forty-niner was not destitute, but after six years he was hardly as well off as he had anticipated when he left New York in 1849.

Columbia, where Churchill spent part of 1852, was one of the richest districts in the southern mines, indeed in all of the Sierra Nevada. Unfortunately for Churchill, the "Gem of the Southern Mines" did not hit full stride until later in the decade, after the period when the unlucky Churchill prospected there.

Included in this section are two letters from Mendal to Charles (April 22, 1852 and February 26, 1854). Churchill always expressed interest in news from home, and Mendal tried to keep up the correspondence despite poor mail service and his brother's propensity for changing his address.

Keystone Furnace Jackson County Ohio

April 22nd 1852

My Dear Brother:

Your letter of Jany 10th came to hand a short time since and we were rejoiced to hear you were still among the living, although I think that trip to Sonora must have nearly did the work. It appears you have not heard from us in a *great while*. I am sorry to have to communicate any bad news but so it is—our Brother-in-law J. F. [Joseph Franklin] Wheeler is dead. He died on the 19th last October with typhoid fever after a severe illness of about 10 days. He was taken sick during court and having a great deal of business to attend to in court did not commence taking medicine soon enough nor taking the proper care of himself untill it was too late. He was a candidate for the office of Probate Judge, and was elected during his illness. His disease settled all in his head and brain and the excitement of court and election was too much for him. He was not in his right mind a great part of the time, and kept talking all the time about elections, lawsuits etc. He had the best medical attendance in reach, and the best care taken of him that could be. His loss on our part is irrepareable. He acquired a great reputation as a Lawyer, and was just beginning to reap some reward for his severe study. He was getting ¾ of the business in court and leaves a vast amount of unsettled law business. It is a severe blow for Melissa, but it was done by him "who doeth all things well." Some three months before Franklin died they lost their eldest child Edward with the flux which was a very severe stroke for Franklin as he thought a great deal of him. That though a severe blow for Melissa, is nothing in comparison to the last bereavement. Melissa has broken up housekeeping and her and her two children are living in Bartons family at Gallipolis. I do not know how the estate will stand but think there will be enough personal property and debts due the estate, to pay all the claims against it, and leave the farm back of Burlington worth some four or 500$ to Melissa and the children. It probably may stand some better than that, but I can not tell yet. Doctor Hall is the administrator and he will settle it up as advantageous as any other man. You say you have not heard from Ohio in 2 years. Well, that is a long time. A great deal transpires in that time. If you have not heard in that time I have written some 5 or 6 letters that you never received. The last I wrote was one in answer to a letter you wrote from Nevada City. I should have written a great deal oftner but you did not keep me posted up as to your whereabouts and when you did write you was nearly always changing places and I did not know where to write to. I left Burlington more than 2 years ago, and have been here ever since. First I went into the store and kept it untill 1st last June, when the clerk sold out and went away, and since then I have been keeping the books of the concern, and am getting a tolerable fair salary. I expect to be able to assist Melissa and mother considerable. By living economical I can save 200$ or 250$ per year. Barton's family live in Gallipolis, and handles the financing of the concern, sells iron, raises money etc.

Mothers health has been good in fact all our family have been tolerable healthy. I have not succeeded in getting Solomon into any good place yet but am on the look out for a place for him. He is here attending the store at this time, but it is only a temporary affair as the store keeper is sick. He has been living with Barton.

The county seat of Lawrence Co. has been removed (or is going to be) to a new town sprung up about 3 miles above Hanging Rock, called, "Ironton." The Iron men about the Rock have jointly built a rail road from their furnaces to the river, the terminus being Ironton. They have a town there of some 15 or 1800 inhabitants, a large Foundry, a rolling mill and a very nice 3 story hotel with some very fine 3 story dwellings all sprung up [within] the past 18 months. About 2 years since the ground [was] nothing but a corn field. Burlington is fast sinking into nothingness. I made my escape just in time. I would not live in Burlington if they would make me a present of the town.

You must write oftener and let me know where you are. Some of us would write you every 2 or 3 weeks if we knew where to write to. I will have Julia write you soon and I shall write soon again. *Don't fail to write often* at *least once in 2 months.* Direct your letter

>Keystone Post office
>Jackson County Ohio
>U.S.

>*Your Affectionate Brother*
>M. CHURCHILL

Received Dec. 24
[Apparently noted by Mendal Churchill]

>Mariposa 31st Oct 1852

Mr. Mendall Churchill

MY DEAR BROTHER

I wrote you from Columbia in answer to your letter of Apl 22d. Since then I have returned from Columbia, and request you to write me at Mariposa instead of Columbia, as I design remaining here during the winter. I have spent considerable time in prospecting latterly and with little benefit to myself. However, I hope to get into some good diggings this winter but am relying almost entirely upon others and I have learned from experience how very uncertain that is.

Since my last, nothing of importance has transpired, excepting that my San Joaquin claims have proved an entire failure, which was very unfortunate for they cost me considerable in cash and labour.

I was wise enough to let the Chowchilla and Frezno[2] alone, notwithstanding that last spring they were supposed to be the best mining districts in Cal. It would have been much better for me if I had let the San Joaquin alone also. Myself together with thousands of others have learned enough to let them alone in [the] future. There is very little gold south of the Mariposa.

I cannot but deeply feel for the loss which Melissa has sustained in the death of Franklin. He was a man of sterling worth and would in a few years have been properly appreciated in Lawrence Co. both as a lawyer and as a man. It also deeply greived me to hear of the death of her oldest child. I hope that Mother continues to enjoy good health. I would be very happy to hear from Julia. I am but a poor correspondent myself. One reason is I lead a very dull monotonous life with but little variety. I can duly appreciate your liberal views with regard to Mother and Melissa. I hope that if I ever get out of this country that I may be able to do something for them myself.

When you write again please tell me how the "Rome folks" get along. Remember me to them when you chance to see them. My best love to Barton and family, not forgetting my little namesake. Also to Barton's Mother who I trust enjoys good health. As I told you before I have but little of interest to communicate whereas you can inform me of many relations and kind friends, which would give me the greatest of pleasure to hear of their prosperity. Please when you write again do not fear of tiring me by the length of your letter. Hoping to soon hear from you

Your Aff Brother
C. W. CHURCHILL

Mariposa 21st Apl 1853[3]

Mr. M Churchill

My Dear Brother

Your letter of 18 Jany has just come to hand & was received with pleasure. I was surprised to hear that you were all in the enjoyment of good health & am happy to assure you of the same with regard to myself. Your remarks about mining are to the letter, and seem as tho' they came from one who had seen the "Elephant." It is useless to regret the past. I can plainly see the reason why I have not made money in this country but I will not attempt to send[?] you a just & sufficient cause for it. I may possibly continue mining in this vicinity next fall, but not after that time. Perhaps I may locate a farm. I am very undecided as regards the future, except in one thing and that is to quit mining. California is certainly the best country for a young man who has to rely on himself to work his way through the world. Though as soon as I can get money enough together, it is my intention to start for Ohio, buy me a farm & marry and live in peace & quietness I think I might make a tolerable farmer after my return, but doubt whether I would be fit for anything else. I will not promise to write you every month, but my letters shall be more frequent than formerly. I lead such a quiet life that were I to write often, I could only give you a bulletin of my health. As for California news I expect you see more of it than I do. Last winter was a very severe one on miners. The heavy falls of rain prevented them from mining & provisions were uncommonly high & very scarce. I paid 50 cents & 60 cents per pound for flour & 75 to 1.00 per pound for pork etc. etc.[4] The diggings in this vicinity are not as rich & as extensive as farther north, but they have their advantages. Viz they are not as thoroughly prospected, neither are there as many miners here as northward. It afforded me pleasure to hear that the affairs of the Keystone furnace are in such a prosperous condition, as Barton is one of the shareholders. What do you think of doing when your engagement expires? I should suppose keeping the Books of a furnace a very desirable situation if the pay is decent. I hope that you will be able to get Solomon a permanent situation where he may learn something that will be useful to him. Does Mother enjoy good health? Your account[?] of news from Rimi [Remi?] was complete, but as it gave me pain to read it I was almost tempted to wish I had not opened[?] it. What is the name of Melissa's youngest boy? and when will she commence housekeeping. Tell Mother that if anything would bring me home it would be to see her. My love to Betsy, Julia & Melissa, not forgetting my little namesake, who must be considerable of a boy. I wonder if Ellen recollects me. I am well acquainted with H. Burton & his wife—please felicitate them (in the usual manner) for me when you visit them. Does H.B. follow the news? Remember me to all inquiring friends & relatives, and altho I refuse to you the monthly articles, there is no reason why you should not write monthly. I promise that you shall hear from me as often as you desire. I heard from Aunt Elizabeth a few days since. She was in fine health.

CWC

Recd Nov 12/53
[Apparently noted by Mendal Churchill]

Mr. Mendall Churchill   Mariposa, 1st Sept 1853

MY DEAR BROTHER

Yours of June 11th was duly received and I owe you an apology for not answering it sooner. Also Julia's letter of 1st May was duly received. Since my last letter I have quit mining and have been clerk in a store on the Mariposa Creek since the middle of May.[5] I shall continue here untill about 1st December, when the store will be closed, as it will not pay to continue the business during the winter. The men with whom I am engaged have two other stores[6] in the neighbourhood, and perhaps I will enter one of them. At all events, I do not think of mining again. If I am thrown out of employment, I would think seriously of returning home. If otherwise I shall remain in California untill I get a little money ahead. I have the entire management of the business in the store where I am employed, and I assure you I have but little leisure time, which is the reason I have not written you before. I was quite pleased to hear of Julia's marriage, and doubt not it will prove a happy one. I was once introduced to Dr. Griswold by Barton, but had no conversation with him. I was very much pleased with what I saw of him. I hope that Barton and Betsey will like Portsmouth, but moving to a new place is always unpleasant. You have to make new friends and acquaintances.

I think it probable you will be able to get Solomon a situation in Portsmouth. I am rejoiced to hear that Mother enjoys such excellent health, and hope that it will long con-

tinue. Burlington must now be a dull place. I never thought
it very lively in its best days. How did Franklin's estate turn
out when it was wound up? If not favorable please let me
know, as you and I are bound to do something for Melissa.
At all events to see her comfortably situated either in Burlington or elsewhere. I am now about 5 miles from Mariposa town, please direct your letters as usual [to] Mariposa.

Sept 16th

I have been so hurried with business that I have not had
an opportunity to continue this letter before the present date.
You can judge for yourself when I tell you that my sales
amt to $100. per day, and that I do a cash business. On Sat-
urday I have a clerk from one of the other stores to assist me,
but the rest of the week I transact all of the business myself.
Most of my customers are Chinamen, a great number of
whom are mining in this vicinity.

Mining in California is now I believe about the poorest
business a man can engage in. Wages are about $3. per day,
and a miner must be tolerable lucky to average that for any
length of time. Of course there are big strikes made occasionally but they are of rare occurrence.

I think it probable that I will be offered the charge of another store as soon as the one I am at present engaged in is
closed. If so you need not expect me [home] next fall. Write
soon and I will end[eavour] to be more punctual in my letters. With Love to all

Your Aff Brother
C. W. Churchill

Keystone Nov. 14, 1853

I received the above letter from Charles on last Saturday and send it to you and the family for perusal. I have written Solomon at Ironton concerning it. So it need not be sent there. Please return after reading etc. as I wish to answer it shortly.

Yours Truly
M. Churchill

The amt. due A McClelland is $119.45

Mariposa 16th Dec 1853

Mr. Mendall Churchill

My Dear Brother

Yours of 28th Aug, came to hand a few weeks since. I wrote you sometime in Sept, which I presume came to hand. I was very glad to hear from you, and particularly as your letter contains no unpleasant news. I am enjoying excellent health, and am still clerking for the same parties, but not at the same place. I am now on the Agua Frio[7] Creek about 5 miles from Mariposa. I am glad that Betsey's health is improving, and hope that her residence in Portsmouth will prove a pleasant one.

The rains have commenced and my employers are getting in large stocks of goods. Provisions will not be as scarce in the mines this winter as the last.[8] The wages which miners make is yearly decreasing but still the mines are overrun with fortune hunters. But few realize fortunes now without much hard labour and perservence in prospecting, together with considerable luck. The old diggings are being worked over and in many instances richer deposits of gold are found in the immediate vicinity of them, than were found when the diggings were discovered some three or four years since. In my immediate vicinity the Chinamen abound, and when I return to Ohio I shall take pleasure in showing you a Celestial Costume, presented me by some of my Chinese friends.[9] You must not be surprised that I send you none but mining news. I have no other. Mariposa County is not as far advanced in civilization as the other mining counties of the State.

The situation which I fill leaves me very little leisure time. When I am not engaged in the store, I am employed in some out-door work. For the first five months my salary was $75. per month, but since then I have received $100 per month, board included of course, particularly as I have to do my own cooking.

I think with you that Aunt Mercy Pritchard and Mr. Haskell make rather an ancient couple, but doubt not it is for the best. When you see David Greene please give him my respects. I am glad to hear that Mr. Wheeler fills the office of Probate Judge. Please remember me to him when you see him. If Melissa wishes to commence housekeeping, I will remit you $100 towards her outfit. If she commences would it not be well enough for Mother to live with her.

The letter which you spoke of writing me, I am daily expecting. I will write you soon again. With Love to all, and my best wishes for your prosperity.

Truly yours etc.
C. W. Churchill

Mendal Churchill. Photograph taken in April, 1863, in Corinth, Mississippi. Photograph courtesy of Mrs. Murray W. Smith.

Mary Loughry Churchill, wife of Mendal Churchill. Photograph taken the day after their wedding on November 29, 1861. Photograph courtesy of Mrs. W. Murray Smith.

Keystone Furnace February 26, 1854

My Dear Brother

Your letter of 16th December 1853 I received a week or
two since. It always affords me great pleasure to receive
your letters, altho you seem to think that as you have not a
whole quantity of connections and friends in California to
write about, that a letter from you is very uninteresting but
that is all a mistake. We are all concerned about your wel-
fare as you are so far away from home, and we are perfectly
willing to pay all postage if it was only to know you were
enjoying good health etc. I have written you one or two
letters, (I do not know certain which,) that you had not
received when you wrote on 16th Dec, but I suppose have
received them ere this. You say you are getting $100 per
month. Well that is just double what I am getting. I should
suppose on that salary you could save 7 or $800 pr annum
but I do not know anything about the expense of living in
California. I know by experience it is a slow way of getting
rich, but I am much pleased to know you have quit mining
and got into something more stable. As from all accounts
and what you wrote also, I consider that a very laborious
and poorly paid occupation, unless a man has extraordinary
good luck.

From the description you give of your occupation I would
not suppose it to be a sinecure by any means but at the same
time it is exchanging an uncertainty for a certainty, and if
it is not so much, you know what you are doing all the while.
Are your employers responsible parties? That is essential,
but it is useless for me to advise you, as I know you have
weathered it around too much to not be wide awake in those
matters. I should like very much to see that "Celestial Cos-

tume" you speak of, and if convenient when you return
bring it along. By the way, when did you think of returning
to Ohio? You say nothing about the time in your last letter.
Barton thinks it would be advisable for you to come home
shortly. My advice is whenever you cease to *do well*, strike
a "bee line" for the States, and I would not stay much longer
in Cal. at any rate I think if I were in your place. We would
all be delighted to see you safe back in Ohio again in "wind
and limb." You know it will soon be 5 years since you left
Ohio, and that is a long time. But about all this you will have
to exercise your good sense and judgement. I wrote you in
my last letter about taking an interest in a new Furnace.
She will commence making Iron in next June or July.

Iron prospects look favorable yet, and a great many
people in this part of the country are paying very high
prices for land for Furnace purposes. That will all do very
well while the price of Iron remains high, but in case it
should suddenly drop, their prices for Furnace property
would be entirely to high. It is hard-telling what's coming,
but I think mine a good investment. I am now engaged making out a Balance Sheet of this Furnace Company and I
think for the past 14 months business they will clear $40,000
or $45,000, but probably these are figures that she will
never reach again. Bartons family like living in Portsmouth
very well. Betseys health is quite good at present.

Melissa, since she has been living in Portsmouth has
learned the Milliner trade, and she and a young lady by
the name of Bartlow, are going to set up shop in Ironton in
a week or two. I think probably she will succeed very well.
Little Jimmy is going to live with his Grandfather, and
Melissa will not set up housekeeping at present, but board

with Joshua Hambleton family, a very wealthy citizen that lived in Burlington when you were in Ohio last. I was not much in favor of Melissa starting out that way, but she seems to desire it, and I thought she might try it, untill she could find something more permanent. I heard a few days ago from Julia. They were well. I also heard the Furnace the Dr. is engaged in made $29,000 on a short blast last year. *Write often*, no matter if your letters are short, we like to know you are "alive and kicking."

Your Affectionate Brother
M. Churchill

P.S. I shall write soon again. Direct your letters as you did the last, Rocky Hill P. O., Jackson Co., Ohio

Mr Mendall Churchill   Mariposa 11th Apl 1854

My Dear Brother

I owe you an apology for not writing you ere this. All that I can say is that I will be more punctual in the future. I received a letter from you some 5 or 6 weeks since, but it has become misplaced and I cannot give you the exact date of it.

I have been in hopes that I would soon receive another from you, but I suppose you are waiting to hear from me. Matters continue the same with me. I shall go in a few days to Mariposita[10] to take charge of a store there, for the same men that I am now with. (It is the place where I stopped last summer). Store's are moved about in California with wonderfull facility. The one to which I am going will be continued only during the summer and fall, and will be a branch of the main store. The past winter has been a severe one [for] the mercantile community. Very little rain has fallen, and the country has been flooded with goods. More than what there were purchasers for. I wish you unbounded success in your Furnace and wish that it was in my power to render you some assistance, but I am husbanding my means with the view to do something for myself should an opportunity occur. With this it was my intention to make a small remittance for Melissa's benefit, but the starting of a branch store by my employer, has rendered the money market rather tight, but it shall not be delayed many weeks.

I hope that mother's health will still continue good, and that Betseys will continue to improve. I lead such a quiet life here that I can have but little or nothing to communicate to you that would be interesting. I presume you are aware that in the mining districts a Merchant has no Sunday's unless he likes to keep Monday. From the commencement of a year untill the close, a store is never closed (for the observence of a particular day). On Sunday we generally do as much business as is done during all of the rest of the week. This is not as it should be and many good men are endeavoring to have the Sabbath observed, but in this part of the country it will be several years before they will suceede in their pious undertaking.[11] I do not know when I shall go home, for at present I think I can do better here than in Ohio, but I wish to make the time as short as possible. I am hoping daily to receive a letter from you not withstanding my own tardiness in writing. Do not delay writing on receipt of this. With love to all

Your Aff. Brother
C. W. CHURCHILL

Rec'd Nov 1st

[Apparently noted by Mendal Churchill]

Mariposa 5th Sept 1854

MY DEAR BROTHER

Yours of 9th July has just come to hand and I hasten to reply. On 24th Aug. I remitted to Cousin William $200. a part of which it will take to pay a debt which I owe in New York. The balance I directed him to forward to you for the use of Melissa. When it arrives please let her have it. It may be of some service to her. I was glad to hear of Mother's recovery and hope that she will continue to enjoy good health.

I am somewhat undecided what to do. I have had several opportunities of engaging in business, but from my experience in merchandising, I have been backward about embracing them. Last spring I came very near going on to the San Joaquin River and engaging in business. It was fortunate for me that I did not, as the business would not have paid as well as I anticipated. I am very glad to hear of your prosperity, and hope the Iron business will continue good. It was unfortunate for me that I came to California, but now that I have remained here so long, I am under the impression I can do better by remaining a short time longer. I am in hopes it will not be long before the Sabbath is respected in the Mountains of California, as well as in the States. The well disposed portion of the Community are moving in the matter. I have remained in the store for 2 months at a time, and never been 100 yards from it, the business requiring my constant presence. In this section of the country we are overrun with Chinese. I have had considerable dealings with them and have not formed a very high opinion of them. It would not surprise me if they were driven out of the Country by the Americans.

How are all the folks at Rome?

Does Barton still own his farm or has he sold it?

Please write soon. I would not have delayed writing as long as I did, only some money which I had out at interest. I could not collect as soon as I anticipated. With Love to all

Truly yours etc.
C. W. Churchill

Sept. 13

I commenced this letter sometime since but have just completed it. A few days since I met a man named Custiss, who says he lives opposite Burlington. He was acquainted with your name, and in fact the whole family. At present he is on the Tuolumne River. I expect him here in the fall. He is talking about returning home soon.

Truly yours etc.
C. W. C.

Mariposa 20th Dec 1854

My Dear Brother

Your letter of 10th Sept came duly to hand, and you probably received one from me of about the same date.

I was glad to hear that Mother's health was improving. Please congratulate Betsey for me on the birth of a son. I hope that Melissa will continue to do well. I expect you

McDermott Tavern (1976). This building, where Churchill apparently died, was known as McDermott's Tavern, later as Gwin Post Office and finally as Union Post Office. Photograph courtesy of Bertha Schroeder.

have received from Cousin Wm. a check for $140.32 for the use of Melissa.

I am very much undecided what to do. I will soon have an opportunity of engaging in business. I can purchase an interest in the house where I now am clerking. If I were to do it, [it] would be very doubtful when I would return. My means are rather limited, and I am of opinion that I can do better in this country with a small capital than at home. The house where I am clerking and of which I have the sole charge has been doing an excellent business for the last 6 months.

The rains have not yet commenced. They are later than usual and everything indicates a dry winter, and if it should prove so, it will make business very quiet. I am sorry that your trade for "Iron Valley" fell through, as I should suppose it an advantageous one for you.

Is Solomon doing business on his own account in Portsmouth, or clerking? I have seen by the papers that money matters were very *"light"* in Ohio, also the failure of some of the Cincinnatti Banks.

With Love to all and hoping there is a letter on the way from you.

Your Aff Brother
C W Churchill

Mariposa 28th Apl 1855

DEAR BROTHER:

Yours of 7th Jany came to hand a short time since and it afforded me pleasure to hear from you and know that you enjoyed good health. Altho much pained to hear of the death of Betsey's Boy, I am glad mother still continues in the enjoyment of health.

My health is excellent. I believe that in the mountains of California (where the Gold Region is situated) it is one of the healthiest countries in the world.

Your prediction in regard to a "General Smash up"[12] has come true with regard to California, as you have doubtless learned from the papers, altho' it has not effected us much up in the Mountains. We depend almost entirely on the mining interest.

With regard to my affairs, I have done nothing definite. The business of the house on a rough settlement did not show as large a profit as was anticipated. Their was a good profit but too much of it was on the books. I think that if things go on right for a short time a branch of this house D. Turner & Co[13] will be opened on the Chowchilla[14] about 15 miles from here and that I will have an interest in it, which I would prefer to an interest in the two other houses—provided that I had the management of it.

I received a letter from Solomon a few days since, which I will answer, directing to Portsmouth.

I hope that it will not be long before you will have a better state of affairs in your section of the country. Hope for the best and try to weather the storm.

With love to all

Your Aff. Brother
C. W. CHURCHILL

106

Mariposa Ranch 1855
Merced Co July 25th

M. Churchill Esqr

Dear Sir:

I am very sorry to have to inform you of the Decease of your Brother C. W. Churchill on the 13th Inst at this place. Charles left the employ of D. Turner & Co., Bridgport, 14 miles from this place about 2 months ago. He paid me a visit of 3 week's after and returned to wind up some business where he spent the 4th. On the 7th he came back very unwell. I procured Dr. Bedford's assistance who waited on him faithfully to the last. Charles was a mutual friend in Augusta, Geo. and more so in this state since 1849. He was in company on the Sonora prospecting trip.[15] I am very sorry to state that while in the above grocer store he was very much abdicted to drinking, also about the 4th which I have no doubt but hurried his last. He was for the last day wandering in mind but conscious of the presence of friends. I can assure you there was nothing wanting that could procure comfort in his last hours. We buried him in sight of the house on an eminence and about 400 yds. [from the house?]. I will get some responsible person to administrate on what can be found of his effects. I think he was getting $1200 pr year from Turner.

You will please write to me on receipt and instruct me what to do and I will cheerfully attend to it.

Yours very Respectfully
WILLIAM LAUGHLIN

P. S. Enclosed you will find a little of his Hair. I retain a little more which I can send on.

W_ML

Address   Quartsburg. P. O.

                  Mariposa Ca

NOTES

1. John S. Hittell, *The Resources of California* (San Francisco: A. Roman & Co., 1863), p. 302.

2. In 1852 there was a small gold excitement on the Fresno River about twenty-five miles south of Mariposa. Frezno was the early spelling of Fresno. The Chowchilla River also had some placer deposits, which Churchill referred to in the letter. His claims were probably on the San Joaquin River, but the district flourished only briefly.

3. This is a pencil copy of the original, written in a hand other than Churchill's. The date and maker of the copy are not indicated.

4. Andrew Church, a Bridgeport merchant during these years, concurred with Churchill about the hard times of the winter of 1852-53. Church, however, had three wagon loads of goods which he had stored and sold at "famine prices." Andrew Smith Church, "Memoirs." *Quarterly of the Society of California Pioneers* (III), pp. 188-89.

5. Churchill made a wise choice: merchants in the mining camps generally made a much better income than the miners — and a steadier one. Miners did not always appreciate the business practices or ethics of the merchants, which led to trouble in several districts. Credit vs. cash payment was one of the major dilemmas facing the merchant in the transitory mining community, where most activities were based on credit.

6. They had stores at Bridgeport, Guadalupe, and Mariposita. Churchill was working at the last one for David Turner and Charles Holt.

7. There was a small bar at Agua Fria Creek, which flourished for a brief time. It is possible that Churchill was at Bridgeport, about five miles from Mariposa. Turner and Holt purchased a store there in July, 1853.

8. The general store in the mining camp had a broad selection of goods; Dame Shirley described one she visited as having the most "heterogeneous

merchandise." There was nothing "you can ask for but what he has—from crowbars down to cambric needles." The quality of the goods was "sometimes rather equivocal." Thomas Eagle pointed out something else about the general store: it was a "boarding house, gambling house, drinking house etc, all under one."

9. Churchill seems to have had a more tolerant attitude toward the Chinese than many other miners of his time, but a subsequent letter of September 5, 1854 indicates that he, too, became more intolerant. A strong current of anti-Chinese sentiment was prevalent in the 1850s. Their appearance at a diggings was seen as a harbinger of decline; according to popular belief, they were able to make a living where a white man could not. Obviously, Agua Fria was well past its peak, as Churchill admits, and the Chinese moved into what were already worked-over districts or leftover claims. The *Mariposa Chronicle*, April 7, 1854, commented, " All China appears to be moving hitherward. The stage comes freighted with loads of Celestials, anxious to pitch into our rich placers, to test the endurance of our miners and to fill our jail."

10. Mariposita was a small placer mining camp on the Mariposa River, active as early as January 1852. Thomas Allsop, writing from there that month, reported a party of Frenchmen had panned two pounds of gold in one day. Allsop felt it was a "first-rate location." In June 1852 American miners drove foreigners from these diggings. Their claims were then auctioned off and mining continued. The incident reflected growing anti-foreign sentiment in California.

Turner & Co. built a store here in April 1854, according to the San Joaquin *Republican*, April 3. The paper called Mariposita a "pleasant little camp."

11. Sunday in the mines was anything but the sabbath of Judeo-Christian tradition. Peter Justesen, who was in the southern mines in the early 1850s, said Sunday was the day he did not work. He went to camp for supplies, hunted, or just loafed. Sunday was a wide-open day in the camps, as ministers soon found out.

12. Churchill was right about the "General Smash up." San Francisco banker William Tecumseh Sherman described it as "the most terrible financial storm that ever devastated any community." On February 23, 1855, seven of nineteen San Francisco banks closed. Other businesses failed and the year was not a good one for the state's major city.

13. David Turner was a Mariposa County entrepreneur. He operated the stores where Churchill worked, owned a quartz mill, and had a financial interest in mines and in the *Mariposa Chronicle*, among other activities.

14. Turner and Holt apparently never opened a store on the Chowchilla. There is no mention of it in county records.

15. Laughlin's name, along with that of John McDermitt who owed money to Churchill's estate, was on the list of names submitted to the Sonoran government in 1851. See the appendix.

VI

EPILOGUE

'Neath an oak beside the mountain,
    Stands a miner's lonely grave,
Near a cool and sparkling fountain,
    Far beyond life's troubled ways;
Now his friends are sadly weeping,
    "Can it be he's dead and gone?"
Yes, in death he now lies sleeping,
    Sleeping gently and alone.

"The Last Good-Bye,"
Golden Songster

Gen. Mendal Churchill (ca. 1890). Photograph courtesy of Mrs. W. Murray Smith.

CHARLES WILLIAM CHURCHILL's quest for his "El Dorado" was finished. His efforts had returned no rich rewards. The shock of his brother's death is evident in Mendal's letter of September 3.

Despite Mendal's worries and Turner's comment, William Laughlin seems to have carried out his responsibilities in settling the estate in a commendable manner. Probate records from Merced County show that Laughlin collected money due the deceased, sold his goods, and paid the few bills against the estate, including some unspecified medicine and medical attendance by one Dr. Bedford in a visit of April 27 and three calls in July. The probate records also show that Churchill continued to look for new ways to make money until the time of his death. In the fall of 1854 he apparently speculated in livestock, for he owed money for "punching, driving and branding" of cattle. When Churchill's debts were balanced against his assets, however, only a modest amount of cash remained for Laughlin to send to the Churchills in Ohio.[1]

Like Churchill, the majority of his contemporaries left no significant legacy. Their significance rests with their total achievement rather than their individual accomplishments. Neither the forty-niners nor their era can be resurrected—and perhaps it is just as well. The frustrations of Churchill are much nearer the norm than the stories of great wealth and a rousing, adventuresome time. For Churchill the frustrations led to drinking, not an uncommon escape when a 49'er saw his dreams evaporating and uncompromising reality staring him in the face. In the aftermath of the news of Churchill's death some relatives reminisced about him; William Churchill, Jr.'s letter of October 9, 1855, especially sheds some interesting light on his cousin.

With the resolution of probate matters, the story of Charles Churchill ends—a brief span of only thirty-two years. But Charles Churchill did not just disappear as so many other forty-niners did. By saving his letters, Mendal Churchill granted his brother a bit of immortality and preserved the memory of a forty-niner who failed.

Keystone Furnace Jackson County, Ohio
Sept. 3, 1855

Mr. William Laughlin

MY DEAR SIR

Your letter of July 25th announcing the very painful intelligence of the Death of my much beloved Brother I received Aug. 31st. The news fell like a thunderbolt on me, particularly that part announcing his habits of dissipation. I thought my Brother was proof against *that* under any circumstances. It is a *great* consolation my Dear Sir to know that he had every attention and comfort in his last hours, and to know that he was attended in his last hours by one he esteemed as a friend, but it seems very hard to die 6000 miles away from home under any circumstances. Please accept my Dear Sir my grateful acknowledgements for your kind attention to him.

You wish me to instruct you what course to pursue in regards to his affairs. Now I do not know anything about your laws, but wish you to settle up his affairs and after paying burial expenses and just debts, if any, remit me the balance if any. If it is any great expense to take out Letters of Administration, the heirs are all of age and they could empower you by power of attorney to settle up his estate for them. We will be governed by your judgments in the matter as you are better acquainted with the customs of that State than we are. If you do not wish to take the trouble of settling up his affairs, I wish you would see that some *responsible*, *honest* man is appointed, but I would much prefer you to administer as I am unacquainted with any one in that country. What will probably be the amount of his effects and liabilities? And of what do they consist?

Of what disease did he die? Did he seem to be aware that his last end was approaching? And did he make any preparations for the final change or wish any word or instruction sent to his family? You will doubtless think I am annoying you with unnecessary inquires, but if so I beg to be excused. You can imagine your own feelings under similar circumstances. If there is a degeaurretype [daguerreotype] likeness of him among his things I wish you would retain it or send it to me by mail and I will fully defray the expenses. Or if it is to cumbersome to send by mail, if you would be coming back to Georgia in a few years I could get it from there if you would have the kindness to take care of it until that time and bring it with you. Or his letters and papers or any little tokens of remembrance that might come into your possession. And I wish you would have the place where his remains are, decently enclosed with some kind of fence or other enclosure and pay for the sum out of his effects. Now my Dear Sir I trust the matter wholly with yourself, thinking it will be done right by one that was an intimate friend of my Brother. Please answer on receipt of this about what arrangements have been made. Address as before, Keystone P.O. Jackson County, Ohio

Yours Very Truly
M. CHURCHILL

P. S. Of course I expect you to pay yourself for whatever trouble you take upon yourself about the matter.

New York Oct. 9 1855

Mr Mendal Churchill

MY DEAR COUSIN,

I have only just received your letter of 2d[?] ult. which sadly confirms what I feared, that Charles is dead.

I grieve to think of it for I was sincerely attached to him. Almost a brother. We were brought up together as brothers. He had the same advantages, the same privileges, the same opportunities for education with myself. If there was any difference, it seemed to be that from his amiable qualities, he won more love, and gained more friends than myself. He had many peculiarities, and we thought sometimes he was somewhat eccentric, but for the pleasure of others, he was always ready to sacrifice his own interests. It was never easy for him to say *No*.

In writing these lines, my memory is running back from fifteen to twenty years, when we were boys together, when the future was bright before us both, and before the clouds of care and "the battle of life" had dimmed our vision or taught us the weariness of the way.

The first intimations I had of this sad event was from my sister, who having been absent in the country for some time, on her return asked me if I had heard from Charles, and told me that a week previous in the California news, had been published the death of "Chas. W. Churchill on Mariposa Creek, aged 26 formerly of Ohio recently of Bridgeport." The age and the "Bridgeport" (which I supposed to mean the city in Connecticut), led me to hope, altho tremblingly that it might not be our Charles. By the first succeeding mail, I wrote to Messrs D. Turner & Co. Mariposa, requesting information and full particulars. As yet there has not been time for me to have an answer. I intended to write to Dr. [?] Griswold but finally concluded not to harrass your minds by our uncertainty and was waiting for news from Messrs Turner & Co. his former employer when your letter reached me today placing the fact of his death beyond a doubt. I never heard of Mr. Laughlin, and rather regret that you had not sent the letter for him to me, when I would have sent it to some responsible parties who would not place him in charge of Charles' effects unless he should be a proper person.

I asked Messr Turner & Co. for an account of his affairs with them, and the condition of his effects, the manner and cause of his death, etc. requesting them, if they held money of his to forward it to me. As soon as I have their answer I will inform you.

When did you last hear from Charles? My last letter from him was dated Apl 28. I had been corresponding with him in reference to his business on the Sabbath and advised him to come home rather than continue in a situation where he must disobey so directly the law of God and desecrate his holy day. Charles, very much to my regret, did not seem to appreciate this evil, but rather extenuated it on account of the condition of society. Why he left Turner & Co. which from Wm. Laughlin's letter, he must have done soon after his letter to me was written, I do not know. I hope they will throw some light upon the subject. The letter of Mr Laughlin is exceedingly unsatisfactory.

Let us not fail to gather a lesson of wisdom from this mournful event, and be ourselves prepared for the summons which sooner or later must come to each one of us. Are you ready? Am I? Momentous questions these. Do you think of them? Mercy is offered now through Christ. Pardon and acceptance with God may now be obtained. Do not slight this solemn warning, my dear Cousin. Do you want a friend that sticketh closer than a brother? Seek and find just such a friend in Jesus.

With much love to your Mother and family and hoping to hear from you again.

I am very truly yours
WM CHURCHILL JR.

Oct 19.

I have this morning a paper from you with the notice of Charles death. I think the age 31 is an error. To the best of my recollection, he would have been 33 years of age, had he

lived until the 23rd of November prox. Some years since,
we had a good deal of discussion on this point, and it was
settled, I believe to the satisfaction of Charles, as I have
stated above.

He died on my Father's birthday, July 13.

Mariposa Ranch
Merced Co 12th Nov. 1855

Mr. Churchill

Dear Sir

Yours of the 3d Sept came to hand in due course. None
regrets more than my self, that your late Bro should have
died so far from all near to him by kindred, and dear by the
ties of affection; but you may rest assured My Dear Sir, that
he died perfectly consious of his approaching dissalution
repentant for past errors, and surrounded by friends who
did all in their power to contribute to his personal comfort.
With respect to his personal and other property, I will my
self administer on his effects. He left some cattle in the hands
of a man in this vicinity, two mining claims in the vicinity
of Bridgport, and an a/c current with his employer D. Turner & Co. On a rough calculation the proceeds may amount
to say $500 less or more. What ever may be the amt I will
see to its recovery. It will most probably be some three mos
before his effects can be turned into cash. It will however be
necessary that I should have from you a power of attorney
to enable me effectualy to act in the matter and I will expect
such communication from you as soon as convenient. His
clothing and some few papers are carefully preserved, but

as to the likeness which you mentioned there is none. As to
the wish you express concerning the enclosure of the place
where your Brother is entered [interred] I shall take care
that it is duly attended to. I remain Dear Sir

Your Obdt Servt
Wm Laughlin

P.S. Direct to Gwin P.O.
      Merced Co
      Cal.

Mariposa Ranch
Merced Co. July 27/56

Mr. M. Churchill

Dear Sir

I am duly in receipt of yours of Jany and Power of Atty.
also yours of May on the 23 Inst. I am sorry I put you to
the trouble of getting the above papers as I applied for Letters of Administration and they were granted me by Probate Court of this county on the 4th Decbr. I have sold at
auction one mining claim for $50.00, 7 head of cattle, one
mule 25.00, pistol 28.00, in all about $410 as near as I recol-
lect, as I deposited the memorandum of sale with County
Clerk. The ballance due by Mr. Turner is about $90, includ-
ing one of the mining claims which he sold. His books was
examined by myself and Justice Vance, one of the apprisers
appointed by Court. Until near Chas. decease they were
kept by him. A cow and calf is unsold yet as she could not
be found. I am confident she will be got and is value about
$57. I have not been able to collect any of the a/c [accounts]

he left nor do I think they are likely to be. They princibly consist of small amts. he loaned and some he went security to Mr. Turner. I think his indebtedness will not exceed $250. You may rest assured that at the expiration of the 10 mos. allowed by law, I will have the matter *settled* and forward to you without delay the proceeds. The completion of Chas. grave will soon be. There were considerable detencion [delays?] with the fences[?]. I will be glad to hear from you on receipt of this and if there is anything you would like to know or enquire about let me know and as far as in my power I will cheerfully comply. Chas. trunk and clothing, papers, etc is carefully stored at Mr. Turner's. Amongst them is a China Dress presented by them to him. Hoping this will be satisfactory I remain yours very Respy.

WM. LAUGHLIN

Gwin P. O.

Gwin Cal Oct 28th 1857

Mr. M. Churchill

DEAR SIR

I am duly in receipt of yours of June and Aug. I could offer you many apologys for my long negligence in remitting you the ballance of the Estate. When I settled with the court I had to deposit the ballance untill I could bring an order from his relative to draw the money. My business and the distance to C.H. and an express office I hope will be ample excuse for my negligence. I hope ere this you have received a check for the amt. and post monie which I had sent by express. Enclosed you will please receive my dis-

charge from court[2] and you will also see the amt. deduct-
ing express expence. I had to get a friend to attend to sending
the check pr mail and the package as I could not leave heare.
I have every confidence he attended to it corectly. I hold the
2d bill or draught. In a short time I will forward you the
bill of accounting[?] in administrating, etc.

Yours very Respectfully
WM. LAUGHLIN

M Churchill Esqr   Agua Fria Dec. 28 1857

DEAR SIR

Yours of Oct 18th came to hand and would have been an-
swered before but for a spell of sickness with which I have
been visited. I was surprised to learn that Laughlin had not
remitted the proceeds of your brother's estate and I know
of no reason why he has not done so.

He is still at the Mariposa Ranch, and is still able to make
the settlement with you, but it is uncertain how long he will
remain able for I understand that he is rather intemperate
in his habits. If you will write to him enclosing your letter
to me I will see that he gets it, and if he then does not render
an account of his stewardship *immediately* I would advise
you to give a power of attorney to someone with instructions
to bring Mr Laughlin to a settlement forthwith. I shall be
happy to render you any assistance in my power in the matter and I think you cannot be too quick in attending to it.

Very truly
Yours etc
D TURNER

NOTES

1. See the document dated January 5, 1857, in the appendix.
2. This document, dated January 6, 1857, is included in the appendix.

APPENDIX A

THE CHURCHILL FAMILY [1]

MARY PRITCHARD (1800) and SOLOMON CHURCHILL (1788); mother and father. Married Union Township, Lawrence County, Ohio, March 16, 1818. Solomon died March 14, 1835, leaving his wife with six children and very little property.

ELIZABETH BARTLETT CHURCHILL

Born September 20, 1820; married to Elisha Greene, Jr. December 27, 1838. Four children were born to Elizabeth before 1849, one of whom had died.

CHARLES WILLIAM CHURCHILL

Born November 22, 1822.

MELISSA CHURCHILL

Born September 18, 1827; married Joseph Wheeler, September 15, 1844. She suffered the double tragedy of having a son and husband die within two months of each other in 1851. Melissa's problems were much on the minds of her brothers.

MENDAL CHURCHILL

Born July 23, 1829. Charles and Mendal were very close, and Mendal was the one who saved the letters that made this publication possible. Much of the support of his mother and younger brother and sister fell to Mendal while Charles sought his fortune.

JULIA CHURCHILL

Born February 25, 1832. Charles could barely have known his sister, as he left home when she was still young.

SOLOMON CHURCHILL

Born July 19, 1834. He was named after both his father and grandfather.

1. Most of this information is derived from a detailed genealogy of the Churchill family, compiled in 1889 by Mendal Churchill. A copy of that genealogy is in the Churchill Collection, San Diego Historical Society.

WILLIAM CHURCHILL
    Uncle of Charles William. Charles worked for William
    Churchill & Co. Lived in New York City.
WILLIAM CHURCHILL, JR.
    Cousin who corresponded with Mendal occasionally. He ap-
    parently was near Charles' age and was married in 1844.

APPENDIX B

MEMBERS OF
THE 1851 SONORA EXPEDITION[1]

THE FORTY-EIGHT MEN listed here, including "Carlos W. Church-ill," journeyed from California to Sonora on a prospecting expedition in 1851:

George W. Hayden
Guillermo Laughlin
Santiago M. Catron
George Bailey
George W. Henry
Juan F. George
Artemas O. Sibley
Patricio Faulkner
Guillermo B. Moody
Guillermo Rooker
Roberto Spurlock
Roberto Henderson
Andrés Jackson
Juan Hutchison
Guillermo E. Hands
David Lauwson
Juan Evans
Guillermo Hauwensten
Guillermo Carr
Juan Elliot
Juan Hester
Suitzer Dentar

Ysac N. Oakes
Daniel E. Bowen
Hiram C. Robison
Guillermo Spurlock
Guillermo Moore
Elijah S. Tasker
Cameron McPherson
Carlos W. Churchill
Miguel Cassida
J. M. Clark
Amos Freeman
Washington B. Smith
Tomás Babington
Ellis D. Holmes
Tomás Gallaway
Juan L. Perley
George Evans
Andrés Lawrence
Adam Bahwel
Santiago Stevenson
Tomás R. Davidson
Santiago C. Wilborn

Signed by Daniel M. Cook, H. B. Bronson, James McDermitt, and Joel Ringo.
July 18, 1851, Ures, Sonora.

1. Archivo Histórico del Estado de Sonora, gaveta 11-1, carpetón 223, expediente 2. A typescript of this document was provided through the kindness of Cynthia Radding de Murrieta, Centro Regional del Noroeste, Hermosillo.

APPENDIX C

SELECTIONS FROM CHARLES CHURCHILL'S PROBATE RECORDS [1]

State of California   SS

County of Merced   KNOW ALL MEN By these presents that William Laughlin as principal and Joseph A. Vance and John James as his sureties are held and firmly bound unto the People of the State of California in the sum of Twelve Hundred Dollars for the same payment of which we bind ourselves our heirs and administrators by these presents.

The conditions of this above obligation is such that whereas the above William Laughlin has been appointed Administrator of the Estate of Charles Churchill Deceased formally of Merced County By the Probate Court of Merced County at a special term held for that purpose on the third (3rd) day of Decr 1855 at the County Seat the town of Snelling in said county

Now therefore if the said William Laughlin shall well and faithfully discharge all the duties of administrator of the Estate of Charles Churchill Deceased as aforesaid, according to law, then this obligation shall be null and void. Otherwise to be in full force & effect. . . . the 4th day of Decr A D 1855

witness   WILLIAM LAUGHLIN [*signatures*]
                  JOSEPH VANCE
                  JOHN JAMES

We the sureties acting as sureties whose names are subscribed to the fourgoing bond Do swear that we are free holders in this

1. The first two documents, dated December 4, 1855, and January 5, 1857, are from the records of the County Clerk, Merced County, California, and form part of Churchill's twenty-five page probate record. Photostats of all the documents are in the Churchill Collection, San Diego Historical Society. The third document, dated January 6, 1857, was sent to Mendal Churchill by William Laughlin and is preserved among the Churchill Letters.

State and that we are worth Double the amount of six hundred dollars mentioned in the above bond over and above our just liabilities.

Sworn to and subscribed before
me this 4th day of December A D 1855

JOSEPH A. VANCE [*signatures*]
JOHN JAMES

State of California   In the matter of the Estate of Charles
County of Merced   Churchill Deceased Before His Hon. I. W.
Fitzhugh Probate Judge for Merced County

WILLIAM LAUGHLIN Administrator of the above Estate would respectfully represent to your Hon. that the following list of property is a true and correct list of all that has come to his hands belonging to said Estate to wit: one pistol, one mule, one Spanish cow, two American cows, and one calf, two Heiffers, and three steers, all of which were sold at the Town of Snelling under an order made by your Hon. and heretofore reported to this Court. The amount of said sales was the sum of $407.00. And also a mining claim which was sold for the sum of $50.00. The amount due the Estate from D. Turner and paid by him $74.04. Amount due the Estate from James McDermott and paid by him $15.00. The Total Amount received by me including all monies paid and all monies received upon sales is $546.04.
The amounts and debts paid out by me is as follows to wit:

Sept 11th 1856 paid Wm Ryan	$20.00
Oct 7, 1856 paid Joseph A. Vance	$20.00
Sept 6, 1856 paid Dr Bedford	$48.00
Oct 18th 1856 paid Thos. R. Murey & Co. [?]	$99.25
Oct 21st 1856 paid Dr. A. D. Boyce	32.00
Oct 20, 1856 paid Laughlin & Js. Dermott	23.00
Nov, 1856 paid for Trunk to send his relatives his clothes	8.50

Amount paid for the pistol of Deceased   28.00
Amount paid Wells Fargo & Co for Transmission
   of the above trunk   18.00
Total Amount paid out by me as Administrator $366.75

Leaving in my hands $179.29 belonging to said Estate out of which is yet to be paid the Expenses of Administration such as the clerks fees, percentage and expenses of Administrator, and Attorneys fees.

And your petitioner Wm Laughlin would respectfully petition your Hon. to order and decree a final settlement of said Estate and discharge your petition and his sureties and will ever pray etc.

Wm Laughlin
Administrator

Sworn to and subscribed before me this 5th day of
January A D 1857

E G Rector, *County*
Clerk

State of California	In the matter of the estate of Charles W.
County of Merced	Churchill deceased, Before his Honor J. W. Fitzhugh probate Judge of Merced County
	January term AD 1857

It appearing to me from the report of the administrator of the above estate William Laughlin and from vouchers filed by him that out of the goods, various[?] chattels, property and debts due said estate, there has come to his hands the sum of five hundred and forty six dollars and four cents and that out of that he has paid the debts of the said Charles W. Churchill deceased and all the expenses of administration amounting to four hundred and fifty two dollars and sixty five cents leaving a balance in his hands of ninety three dollars and thirty nine cents which he has

131

this day paid into the court to await the order of the brothers and heirs of said deceased. And it further appearing to me from said report and petition of said administrator to be discharged that he has justfully and correctly administered the estate of said deceased.

It is therefore ordered and decreed that the said William Laughlin and his surities be and are hereby discharged and in conformity with the prayer of said petition the final settlement of the administration of said estate is this day ordered and decreed.

January 6 AD 1857

> J. W. FITZHUGH *Probate Judge*
> *Merced County*

State of California   }   SS
County of Merced

I, E. G. RECTOR

County Clerk of said county and state do hereby certify that the above decree is a true copy of the Original now on file in the probate court of said county

In witness whereof I have hereunto set my hand in seal of office at the town of Snelling on this 12th day of April AD 1857

> E. G. RECTOR *County Clerk*
> *and Ex oficio Clerk of the Probate Court of M Co*

Filed on the 6th day of January AD 1857 E. G. Rector Probate Clerk *M Co*

FOR FURTHER READING

The following list is not intended to be all inclusive, rather it is designed to provide further sources for understanding California mining of Churchill's day and to serve as a starting point for an enjoyable literary trip back to the days of forty-nine.

Borthwick, J. D. *Three Years in California.* London, 1857.

Caughey, John. *Gold is the Cornerstone.* Berkeley, 1948.

Clappe, Louise. *The Shirley Letters.* New York, 1949.

Delano, Alonzo. *Alonzo Delano's California Correspondence.* Sacramento, 1952.

Dwyer, Richard A. and Richard E. Lingenfelter. *The Songs of the Gold Rush.* Berkeley, 1964.

Hittell. John. *Mining in the Pacific States.* San Francisco, 1861.

——————————*The Resources of California.* San Francisco, 1863.

Johnson, William Weber. *The Forty-Niners.* New York, 1974.

Justesen, Peter. *Two Years' Adventures of a Dane in the California Gold Mines.* Gloucester, 1865.

Kemble, John H. *The Panama Route, 1848-1869.* Berkeley, 1943.

Kip, Leonard. *California Sketches with Recollections of the Gold Mines.* Albany, 1850.

Marryat, Frank. *Mountains and Molehills or Recollections of a Burnt Journal.* New York, 1855.

M'Collum, William. *Califorrna as I Saw It.* Buffalo, 1850.

Paul, Rodman. *California Gold.* First ed., 1947; Lincoln, Neb.; 1964.

——————————*Mining Frontiers of the Far West 1848-1880.* New York, 1963.

Pierce, Hiram D. *A Forty-Niner Speaks.* Oakland, 1930.

Royce, Sarah. *A Frontier Lady.* New Haven, 1933.

TAYLOR, BAYARD. *Eldorado, or Adventures in the Path of Empire.* New York, 1949.

WHEAT, CARL. *Books of the California Gold Rush.* San Francisco, 1949.

WOODS, DANIEL. *Sixteen Months at the Gold Diggings.* New York, 1851.

Index

Compiled by Duane A. Smith

No 1.

Steamer Crescent
Received   149.   Sunday 8th

Dear Brother
                    I wrote you on 29th
New York, of my hasty departure for
Tomorrow I expect to reach Chagres,
with no detention at Panama, shall re
by middle of August. This vessel saile
all — + by hard work I got aboard a
before she left the dock — I was so mu
that I had no time for reflection, regr
although I felt some when fairly emb
my voyage — but now I have recove
spirit, + feel more sanguine of succe
efore I started, I have enjoyed excellen
+ we have had but one warm day s
left New York, + that was soon afte
the sun's line — now we are going s
he sun + the weather will not gro
as you might suppose. I have a s
passage on this vessel for which I p
+ steerage ticket on the Pacific side
I paid $180. — the expense of crossi